Light Your Spiritual Passion

Laura Lee Perkins

Inspirational Essays to Inspire a Quickening of the Soul

Lighting Your Spiritual Passion

© 2013 Laura Lee Perkins
P.O. Box 37 / Searsport, ME 04974
www.LauraLeePerkinsAuthor.com

ISBN-13: 978-1-938883-76-7

All rights reserved. No part of this book my be reproduced in any form or by any electronic or mechanical means, including information storage and retrieval systems, without permission in writing from the author, except by a reviewer, who may quote brief passages in review.

Designed by
Sharon L. Power
12431 N. 22nd Ave., Phoenix AZ 85029
602-997-9777 • powgr5@cox.net

Produced by
Maine Authors Publishing
558 Main St. Rockland ME 04841
www.mainauthorspublishing.com

CONTENTS

Preface	....	iii
Chapter 1	Learning Life's Lessons	1
Chapter 2	Remembering Our Sacred Contracts	9
Chapter 3	Life Leads Forward into LOVE	17
Chapter 4	How Does God Appear?	23
Chapter 5	Closer Encounters with Self	27
Chapter 6	Answering Our Needs	33
Chapter 7	The Circle	39
Chapter 8	The Power of Forgiveness	45
Chapter 9	Finding God at the Beach	53
Chapter 10	Clearing Clutter = Making Space for Spirit	57
Chapter 11	Moving Forward into Center	65
Chapter 12	Opening into Spirit	73
Chapter 13	Honoring Completion	83
Chapter 14	Growing in Spiritual Unity	89
Chapter 15	Love Is One Mind, One Heart, One Soul	95
Chapter 16	Lighting Your Spiritual Passion	101
Chapter 17	Marrying the Personality and the Soul	109
Chapter 18	Feeding the Soul with Reverence	117
Chapter 19	The Love We Give Away Is the Only Love We Keep	125
Chapter 20	The Mystic Map Within	131
Chapter 21	The Fountainhead	137
Chapter 22	How Is Your Spiritual Nature Connected to Your "Real" Life?	143

i

Preface

Preface

Lighting Your Spiritual Passion inspires a quickening of the soul, which yearns to meld with the personality, enabling us to fulfill our purpose here on earth. This process involves learning that the only Love we keep is the Love we give away. As our soul quickens in response to moments of grace, it expands through illumination and our spiritual roots grow deeper into the soil of life.

This collection of twenty-two inspirational essays is filled with many experiences that have brought light into my soul. *Lighting Your Spiritual Passion* explores the mystery of life and the human desire to experience transcendence. I believe that spiritual guidance, flowing up and out of our deepest wells of intuition, is available to all seekers who are willing to make a commitment to the personal spiritual journey process. Each person must choose a path that feels comfortable, and this book is written to be inclusive of your personal spiritual path. You will encounter many terms that refer to the Divine: Light, Spirit, Infinite Intelligence, the ALL, Force, Universal Intelligence, Source, and God.

It is my desire to touch the reader on many levels. Therefore, the essays are easily accessible to both those who are beginning their spiritual exploration and those who have traveled on a long spiritual quest. Because the book is written in essay format, you can open the book to any chapter at any time. As food for the mind and soul, it can be a bedside companion, a coffee-table book, or a text to use for group spiritual exploration and discussion. My desire to share personal spiritual expansion experiences comes from a deep level of love and caring for all.

Lighting Your Spiritual Passion honors the magnificent inspirational power of nature as you travel to a variety of locations with me. In one chapter, you will feel the heat of the campfire as I nestle into the bank of the Colorado River. In another chapter, you will travel with me on a journey to search for ocean sea glass—and discover God—which you might call by another name. The Divine animating power of everything has many possible names, so use one that feels comfortable to you.

As a worldwide community of individual souls, we share a connected experience. Enveloped in an evolutionary process, we are moving out of our historic communal past, which has been filled with epic sagas of conquer and destroy. We are transitioning into a pilgrimage of Healing Light, slanting across our landscape. Discussing the elimination of guilt and fear— the two emotions that can freeze—helps to transform these emotions, freeing us, through the experience of grace, into a life that is filled with passion and excitement about the future.

This book attempts to feed your soul with reverence and your mind with knowledge that enhances awe. The writing

Preface

encourages mediation, which involves respect, while embracing flexibility and vision. As an example, this book explores betrayal and hurt as gifts, because they can propel us forward into the process of forgiveness.

Spiritual work is radical; it is often painfully deep and searching. It is a long process requiring commitment and elasticity, but the rewards are internal peace, forgiveness, love, and bounteous joy. My intent is to lead you on a quest to explore what lights your spiritual passion. You might want to pause and reflect after reading each essay. Hopefully, these essays will nudge you, through sensitive and thoughtful dialogue, into deeper levels of spiritual trust, resulting in an expanded, more dynamic zest for life.

> My entire life has felt infused with spiritual energy.
> As a child, I always knew that I was protected
> and guided by an inner voice.

> Spirit lives in every cell in our bodies, and we can access
> this magnificent and loving Force at any time.
> Spirit is always available.

CHAPTER 1

Learning Life's Lessons

Chapter 1

Learning Life's Lessons

There are countless approaches to living a life. Many people want to just survive, to make their way to the goal, which seems to be death. Some want to live a life filled with learning, while others want to earn lots of money. Some folks lie and steal, some folks tell the absolute truth, but most live somewhere in between these two poles. The one thing that is constant is our searching nature. We were given an intelligent and curious mind so that we can both search for our ancestral roots and attempt to peer forward into our veiled future.

The steps along the path of life are strewn with experiences that are often referred to as "life's lessons." Is it important that we learn new ways of being in the world? I believe it is. Following are some ideas and concepts that have been meaningful to others. Perhaps these might be worth contemplating for your own personal development and growth.

Many inventors have written about the importance of an active listening mode, when ideas flow from some invisible source to the surface of consciousness where they can be used. Is this power source internal or external? I believe it is both.

This power that exerts itself to be recognized is beyond

what most of us can conceive, yet we often feel it stirring within us. For some, it perhaps sounds odd to think about listening to oneself, but this is an important skill to cultivate because our inner dialogue is often repetitive and nonproductive. Learning to "get clear" as we listen to our inner voice allows us to tap into new ideas that are moving toward our awareness—moving into the Light where we can understand and implement their wisdom. The animating flow that propels information into our consciousness is both within us and external. It is information and awareness that rises into conscious thought and comes from sources to which we are connected. The flow of a creative life is from the inside out. The flow's source is the animating energy of pure Spirit, which dwells both within and without; it is immersed in the ALL.

There is one mind common to all; we have direct access to it and we can use it for good. This is the "consciousness of Spirit"—or one might call it the "mind of God." It is the Universal Intelligence that has created us as we are in this very moment. And it exists as a power outside of ourselves, to whom we can talk or pray, and within ourselves, where we can go in meditation to access our Higher Self—that part of us possessing the ability to creatively process new concepts.

Accessing Universal Intelligence means coming into an alignment where vibratory frequencies are compatible. In a symphony orchestra, when the concertmaster sounds the tuning pitch A, vibrating at 440 decibels per second, all orchestra members tune by matching that same vibratory speed for the same pitch. The process works in the same manner when we strive to align our energy with the Universal Intelligence. Only when we are in harmony with information we are attempting

Learning Life's Lessons

to access, can we open a clear channel to receive it. The information is always there, and it is always available, but we must alter our internal vibrations so that our minds can become receptive vessels. This is one of the purposes of meditation: to clear the mind of cluttering energies so that the speed and clarity of the information flows into the mind in ways that we as humans can comprehend.

We have access to all of the tools that we require to live in harmony upon this truly magnificent planet. Isn't that an amazing concept? We can learn new ways of moving toward peace, rather than constantly preparing for warfare. We can learn to be actively engaged in the process of determining what is in the highest and best interest for all. One person at a time, we can expand the intention of a committed desire for world peace.

Things that we give our attention to are quickened with new energy. Anything that we focus on, whether it be positive or negative, pulsates with increased aliveness when we offer it our attention. By choosing our focal points very carefully and being open to receive entirely new ways of doing things, we can transform negative into positive, which is *always* in our highest and best interest.

Forming a partnership with Spirit will bring you prosperity in many ways; aligning self with the creative force offers a full bank of opportunities. Our choices in life expand as we are empowered by spiritual connectivity. Our personal thirst for more can only be satisfied by following the internal spiritual river back to its source. We are immersed in spiritual power that is available for us to use.

In preparing for your journey—your arrival back into

LIGHTING YOUR SPIRITUAL PASSION

conscious connection with the Source—it might be helpful to consider that Spirit's qualities already exist in your being. These qualities, such as love, compassion, and intelligence, show up in many ways in your current daily life. By becoming more aware of these moments of spiritual contact, you can choose to broaden and expand them. When you have a "hunch" that just keeps gnawing at you, or when you seem to be "in the flow" with repeating synchronistic experiences, you are definitely in alignment with spiritual connections.

Think about a time when you have been through an experience where you felt particularly strong or courageous. That is an example of tapping into your own spiritual strength, which is intensified by simply honoring it. There are times when our own feelings of compassion seem overwhelming, and we offer some unexpected kindness to help another. Here again, spiritual energy, expressed as love, propels us into action. This is another opportunity to see a quality of the Source expressing itself through us. We are God's physical means for expression on earth; contemplate that responsibility!

When we have an intuitive feeling or hunch about something, when we feel drawn to move in a new direction, Spiritual Light is guiding us through our intuition. These "intuitive leadings" (as the Quakers call them) fill us with joy when we follow their nudges. I believe that Spirit truly wants us to be filled with happiness—joyful celebration—as we move deeper and deeper into trust. The process is slow but thorough as long as we stay on the path of spiritual exploration. Humans have an innate need to explore where we have come from and where we are going. Sometimes we try to slide backwards into uncertainty and unknowing, but the more one moves forward,

Learning Life's Lessons

guided by spiritual inner promptings, the more serenity and peace appear to fertilize our life's growth.

As we put down deep roots into the fertilized soil of trust, we begin to see beauty everywhere we look. It is in everything, and the beauty is constantly unfolding and changing. We begin to embrace awe. We stop dancing with ghosts to music that is no longer playing. We leap into creative action, often after years of indecision, and we learn to waltz with God to music we can now hear playing.

CHAPTER 2

Remembering Our Sacred Contracts

Chapter 2

Remembering Our Sacred Contracts

Spiritual work is about the exploration of mystery and the desire to experience transcendence. That is why spiritual works feels so magnetic; the power of the draw is unexplainable at times. We yearn to learn more and more and more about how we have come to walk upon this earth. Where have we come from and why are we here? Did we make an agreement—a sacred contract—to be born? If so, how can we explore our purpose here on earth?

Our communal historic past often seems pretty grim in hindsight. Yet there are slivers of Divine Light that peek through the window of human history, and that Light is beginning to slant in new directions. Centuries of plundering and conquering for egotistic purposes fill the books of our human records. But we are beginning to view life differently as we slowly creep toward a consciousness of unity. Are we beginning to remember some sacred contracts that were set up before we came to earth? I believe this is true.

When folks remember a Near Death Experience (NDE), they commonly report moving through a dark tunnel and coming in contact with spiritual entities who appeared either out of, or surrounded by, light. They clearly remember telepathic conversations that include life reviews encompassing the concept of fulfilling a "life purpose" they had seemingly agreed to before birth. These reports are not unusual but are the norm for those surviving a NDE, and they report that their personal contracts were often "reviewed" during a NDE. If the person needed more earthtime to complete their mission, they often describe being told that they were being sent back. And suddenly they were transported back into their physical body with a rapid *whoosh* feeling.

Form has always held value. Form offers us a level of structure that we can begin to comprehend because it is organized. A contract could provide an agreed-upon form for a soul returning to earth. Form allows us to have an alphabet that can be shaped into words. Architects provide printed diagrams and plans of how we can form physical materials into living and working spaces, and churches provide structured edifices for worship. Libraries and academic institutions, as well as museums, offer us the value of form (organized materials) for edifying and codifying our learning.

Yet it is important that we not get stuck within the form but use it as a springboard to further understanding. There can be a paradox here if the form is considered to be the final destination. It is not. The form (or structure) is the foundation of support. A life contract only provides the intent of achieving the contract's stated goal. We might have the purest intention, for instance, of learning about a particular subject in great depth in order to become a wealth of inspiration and information for others. Yet there is more—there is the magnificent opportunity to *create* out of the form...to bring more awareness forward.

Remembering Our Sacred Contracts

As a musician, I am reminded of the years of theoretical music learning that I have experienced. For instance, harmonic compositions in the earliest years of polyphony often moved from the tonic (I), to subdominant (IV) to dominant (V), allowing for modulations and cadence points. This common I-IV-V pattern, while important in the foundational structure of elementary harmonies, becomes extremely repetitious and boring when it is repeated over and over. However, when composing a "new" musical composition, it is very important not to simply recreate the forms that we have studied so carefully. These structured elements become the foundation for future creativity; one must have the necessary musical tools to write down the notes. But these notes will be compiled in new and meaningful ways to bring more new music into the world. Many composers say that the notes "come to them" from spiritual inspiration, just as a painter might be spiritually inspired to paint the same scene that other painters have attempted. But this particular artist might paint it using different colors, paints, or brush strokes, resulting in a new interpretation of a familiar scene. Spiritual inspiration arrives cloaked in many different garments!

As we open to spiritual guidance while retaining some semblance of form for spiritual access (meditation, prayer, exercise, etc.), we might be led or induced into higher levels of consciousness. The experience of this creative motion is similar to falling in love, because we are learning about the essence of the love out of which we were born. Spiritual connectivity can feel very much like falling in love, allowing us to experience deep levels of trust and risk-taking. When we fall in love, our previous judgments are often thrown to the

LIGHTING YOUR SPIRITUAL PASSION

wind and we see God in the eyes of our beloved—who might have stringy, dirty hair and no taste in personal dress. When we love, we are blinded by the faith of that experience. When we love, we have courage—we feel strong and powerful through that love connection. Spiritual connections can also make us feel more courageous, strong, and empowered. Why? Because spiritual connections offer us a taste, a glimpse, of the Divine. God is Love.

Also, that which inspires our curiosity draws us deeper and deeper into its awareness. If we are curious about spirituality and just cannot seem to stop thinking about it, we are being summoned to learn more. There is a gift in this summoning— the gift of grace! As we respond to the calling, we shall be led (by what we commonly call our intuition) into opportunities that would previously have been beyond our imagination. Motivated by Spirit, our intention, coupled with our curiosity, motivates us to keep moving deeper into our spiritual discernment. The power of our commitment to this intention will equal the power of the results we uncover in this experiential process. As we search for answers internally, the process is similar to a computer search: we are looking for what we are going to manifest. As we deepen our trust in spiritual guidance, we rise into more elevated states of connected consciousness.

When we become immersed in—or joined with Spirit— our internal vibration accelerates. This change involves an increase in the vibrational frequency (rate per second) as we are moved from one level of vibration (physical/visible) to another (spiritual/invisible). We grow beyond that which we were able to first imagine. Then we can live and work at that new frequency for a time, until we are spiritually prepared to advance again. As we transform from one frequency into the next higher level, our life's purpose becomes more and more clear, and the spiral of spiritual connection expands to touch more and more people. Our life's path is a natural, upward spiral as we develop a closer relationship with our Higher Power.

We truly will blossom through offering ourselves to purposeful (God's) work. When we offer to open ourselves spiritually, our lives begin to unfold—to open—in ways that seem filled with purpose and reverence, and we are truly transformed. If you feel inhibited about understanding your life's purpose or stuck in your spiritual progress, then explore that feeling deeply to understand what is holding you back. What would it take to move you into deeper faith? Ask for it, but do not beg. Set your intention.

The Creator transformed nothing into something with a thought; because we are made in the Creator's image, we too have the ability to create with our thoughts. Isn't that an awesome idea—that with our own thoughts, we can create? SOME THINGS HAVE TO BE BELIEVED TO BE SEEN. And the invisible is more potent, more powerful, than that which can be seen.

Once spiritual movement and expansion begin in our soul, animating and exciting as it is, we form a closer spiritual connection with the Divine! The thrill of the experience stays within our awareness, and we can never go back to being uncertain about spiritual presence in our lives. We know that we have help available—always—no matter how difficult things might become. We trust that we are made in the image of God = Love.

CHAPTER 3

Life Leads Forward into LOVE

Chapter 3

Life Leads Forward into LOVE

How are you walking this path of life? Are you open to love or are you afraid that you might not be up to the challenge of giving and receiving love?

Many of us live with a pretty high level of fear on a daily basis. We are afraid that we might get sick, or we are afraid that we were unkind to someone or that we will not have enough money. We might fear losing our job; maybe we fear being incompetent at our jobs. When we are students, we might fear that we cannot earn the grades necessary to graduate or to complete the learning process that we need to have our dream job. How can we move past this daily impediment of fear?

One way is by honoring rituals in our lives. We came to earth to fulfill a sacred contract, and we use rituals to celebrate, mark, and remember what is important to us in this process of contract fulfillment. Rituals help us continue to grow in our search for spiritual connections because they help us to focus, remind us of God's presence, offer symbolic ways to express remorse and gratitude, and offer completion. Whether it is a baptism, a wedding, a graduation, or a funeral, ritual marks the event as special, as an honoring.

LIGHTING YOUR SPIRITUAL PASSION

We can use rituals to draw spiritual power closer to us through worship, prayer, and thanksgiving. All of these rituals demonstrate trust in a spiritual power that is greater than ourselves. While fear *shuts* the gate to Love, trust *opens* the gate. When we trust, we know that the gate to Love will be opened in the right way and at the right time. As children and young adults, we often participate in rituals designed by others. However, as adults exploring deeper connections in personal spiritual experiences, rituals can be strengthened if you design them yourself (rather than creating carbon copies of others' rituals), thereby demonstrating your willingness to be led by Spirit. Using your own creativity, write your own prayer ritual or create a special celebration ritual to invite and honor Spirit.

Prayer is hope in action with no boundaries, and prayer can happen at any time in any place. Prayer demonstrates trust as long as we do not use it to beg, but instead use it to simply put our soul into alignment with our own spiritual values. As we deepen our relationship with God through prayer, we learn about patience and persistence; we learn how to wait without fear. That is a huge leap forward! Prayer doesn't change God, but it does change us. We learn to take an active role in moving through personal hurts, allowing the unseen path into the future to unfold, as we learn to understand more about our own personal expectations and our relationship to the Divine.

We have the ability to reflect and prayer can facilitate that reflection, moving us into deeper caverns of understanding as we unfurl our beautiful petals of Love out into the world. Prayer doesn't change the Almighty or the angelic spirits who assist us here on earth, but it does help us to choose trust over fear. When we offer prayerful gratitude, our lives become a creation

Life Leads Forward into LOVE

rather than a reaction and we are strengthened. This sense of empowerment enables us to face life's obstacles and challenges.

When we are faced with obstacles, only one thing makes the difference: the willingness to accept the responsibility to move forward. Over time, our desire to move forward, to be closer to Spirit, and to live in the constant presence of LOVE teaches us to make decisions in different ways. We learn when to hold back and when to push, and we feel more love toward all. Life is no longer about "us and them." We connect with the divine nature in ourselves, and we perceive that divinity in others. We feel connected to every thing and to every one. We no longer have a sense of isolation and loneliness because WE KNOW LOVE.

How are you walking this path of life? Are you open to love? Do you live from a position of fear? We are always moving forward on the path of life. Whether we do so in fear and accept all the trouble that fear brings us, or whether we choose to embrace LOVE and the benefits love brings us, is our choice. It is up to us. Through our rituals, especially prayer and meditation, we can choose to make our walk hand in hand with LOVE.

CHAPTER 4

How Does God Appear?

Chapter 4

How Does God Appear?

If we are the creative outlet through which God's presence manifests in the world, then what happens if our own creative impulses become blocked? How is the energy to be released? How is God's presence to be made known? Keeping the channel open, free-flowing, and unobstructed is our personal challenge. The process is not about bringing things in, but of releasing the information that we hold, in our sacred internal space, from the inside out.

We were born with the capacity to trust, to have faith that goodness will flow. But we can learn to be fearful, to shut off the flow of information that comes to us through intuition and spiritual connections. We can build internal dams or have severe internal spiritual drought. We can live with hope for a bright future or we can live within the fear of past hurts reappearing in our lives. Our attention magnifies any of these circumstances; where is *your* attention?

We were born with free will, and we have the freedom to choose to approach life from either a negative or a positive stance. Any form of negative attention brings more negativity. When we are in a condition of fear, anger, or worry, our Divine

LIGHTING YOUR SPIRITUAL PASSION

Energy, instead of flowing, becomes dammed up within ourselves. We all know people who think in negatively destructive ways; it is only by being vigilant about our own thinking (and speaking) patterns that we are able to keep our internal rivers open, allowing Spirit to flow freely. This approach magnifies the positive energy in any and all situations.

It is all right to experience discontent, because discontent forces us to look at our lives more realistically. Discontent can lead us into more positive responses. Sometimes it is very enlightening to be discontented with the state of things if that state includes dullness, failure, frustration, or loss of hope. The exploration of discontent can be the impetus that spurs us into action. Just because we have chosen to analyze our discontent does not mean that the evaluation process should involve negativity.

When we feel called into service by spiritual forces, when we believe that there is truly a way for us to be in the world that brings contentment, everything will be furnished to pave that way as long as we stay with our committed intention to walk a path of spiritual connection. Knowing that spiritual support, guidance, and comfort are always available for the asking eliminates so much fear from our lives. That does not mean that "finding our life's purpose" and living from a position of positive trust will just be handed over to us without our having the necessary commitment and doing the required work. Knowing that the resources necessary to fulfill the calling will be offered when we are ready changes everything. Emmet Fox writes of these things in his book *Power Through Constructive Thinking*, in which he says, "Your Heart's Desire is the Voice of God, and that voice must be obeyed sooner or later." Listen to the voice in your heart to keep the inner wisdom channels open.

CHAPTER 5

Closer Encounters with Self

Chapter 5

Closer Encounters with Self

Ernest Holmes, the founder of *Science of Mind*, wrote much about our unity with the Creator. In his writings, we read about the primary importance of inclusion in our thinking. Holmes believed that a finely honed philosophy came from inclusive thinking and embracing the concept of unitary wholeness. Simply defined, this means that all things with a life force on earth have a spiritual connection to one another. Without this connection, he says, there is "inconsistency in our thinking and instability in our consciousness."

If we are truly one with all of creation, then everything that we do is an expression of the Creator; it is our choice as to exactly HOW we bring the Creator into the world. Confidence and conviction bring more clarity and goodness forward because it is in the expectation of confidence and conviction that clarity and goodness are created. Fear and doubt bring confusion. Placing blame causes us to become stuck. Being open to internal change is about making a conscious choice, through rational thinking, to allow our spiritual nature to unfold and expand. Rational thinking is therefore spiritual.

LIGHTING YOUR SPIRITUAL PASSION

If we believe that the Great Spirit wants to actively sustain and support this earthly life experience, then being open to strengthening closer encounters with Spirit is in our best interest. Living from a belief that trusts in spiritual communication enhances the quality of our lives. Every single day, we have the opportunity to be reborn within, we have an opportunity to form a closer relationship to Spirit. Being open to new opportunities for expanding spiritual connections daily serves us well.

Are you open to an evolving, maturing concept of Spirit and how that energy manifests within your own life? Is the Great Spirit your best friend in times of celebration and in times of trouble? Do you experience joy and comfort from the relationship? Is trust the basis upon which you continue to grow in Spirit? If you can honestly answer "yes" to these questions, you have a strong spiritual foundation.

Flexibility is the key to the door of spiritual connection. It is impossible to make God conform to our own preconceived notions. The connections with Spirit are unlimited when we unlock our ego, which is what separates us from Spirit. Living from an egotistical stance requires that we think of ourselves as isolated and separate. Living from within a spiritual base of unity consciousness allows us to perform meaningful work within the world while operating from a position of love and compassion.

Operating from this base does not mean that we will not suffer. Suffering brings new learning into our lives because it opens us to the Holy Spirit and to the experience of grace. Feeling uncomfortable is a sign that we need a tune-up, that our internal spiritual engine needs a cleaning or an adjustment. Discomfort is like a ringing phone beckoning us to answer it, to pay attention, because someone is calling.

Closer Encounters with Self

If there is a telephone line in spiritual work, then God is the caller and our conscience is the telephone line. When we answer, the voice we hear comes from the God-force moving within us. But whether or not we choose to answer the ringing is up to each one of us. If we answer, do we listen to the voice? The struggle is often between answering the call immediately after the first ring or deciding to answer after several rings, when we can no longer deny or ignore our impulse to respond.

It is often said that we cannot see the answers directly in front of us, but must ask others for advice. Perhaps this is because we have not learned how to really listen to our inner voice. Living from a truly authentic stance is very creative; living a life that is filled with doing what others expect is reactionary. Are we truly observing our own lives, or are we living a fairy-tale existence? Do we understand our impact on others, or are we spending too much time thinking about their impact on us? Are we burdened by how we think things *should* be rather than by how things actually are? Most every day is filled with opportunities; are we being cognizant? "Know thyself," we often hear, and how true it is!

Our societies have spent centuries trying to conquer and master the plant, animal, material, and human world. Is this for the betterment of humankind? Certainly that was part of our ancestors' intentions, but the world still suffers. Have we been diligent caretakers of our fragile planet, which supports all life as we know and experience it? How can we do better? If we believe in a Higher Power and tap into the strength of Divine guidance, we have the opportunity to open the channel of connectivity and healing for the entire planet. We have an opportunity to move beyond war and conflict into peace.

CHAPTER 6

Answering Our Needs

Chapter 6

Answering Our Needs

We all have felt forsaken and abandoned by God at some time in our life. We have each experienced the sense of aloneness that shakes the very foundation of our inner core. During these times of confusion and loss we wonder, "Why has God abandoned me? What have I done to deserve such pain, such a sense of isolation, such a loss of hope?"

The problem is not in God's willingness to become involved with us. Spirit is always present and available. The problem is that we, in our humanness, often have difficulty accepting this universal Divine Presence as a reality of life.

When we are asking for intervention to change a situation, what we often really need is comfort to accept what is. The Divine Presence within us can be utilized to help comfort and inspire us, but we must summon it into action. By asking through prayer, we show a level of trust and agreement to act in concert with the response. Sometimes we simply need to ask for the patience to wait; change is the one constant in all difficult situations.

We all want to be happy, to enjoy good health, and to be prosperous. We want to have friends and to have opportunities

LIGHTING YOUR SPIRITUAL PASSION

to contribute something toward the betterment of mankind. The ways in which we tap into the power to realize our dreams are many and varied, but all begin with believing that realization of our dreams is possible. This knowledge gives us a sense of permanent rooting. Knowing that there is an underlying, pervasive power that flows through us, connects every living thing, and is always available brings great satisfaction. That power is always present within each of us. It can lie dormant year after year or we can activate it and use it on a daily basis. Which do you choose?

In his voluminous writings, Ernest Holmes described this invisible essence of nature as goodness, truth, wisdom, beauty, energy, and imagination, and he said that our highest satisfaction comes from a sense of conscious union with this essence. In other words, trusting in an Infinite Intelligence as a singular power underlying all life brings satisfaction.

When we are able to align ourselves with this Divine Energy, we find an inner wholeness that dissipates all fear, doubt, and uncertainty. When trust dissolves feelings of aloneness, isolation, and abandonment by God, you can begin the process of becoming that small beacon of light that begins to illuminate others' lives. You can be a little flame in the darkened rooms of despair, loss, and aloneness. You can illuminate the spaces where others will have a glimpse of Spirit at work in your life. You can be the example that leads others into the space of experiencing God's omnipotent presence.

The recognition of our connection to Spirit expands one's life. When we act on this recognition, God becomes realized. When we acknowledge the goodness of God, we experience a sense of inner peace. This spiritual essence is the animating

Answering Our Needs

principle that operates through every living thing—even a blade of grass. The Talmud states, "Every blade of grass has its angel that bends over it and whispers, 'Grow, grow.'"

We bring individual personalities to Earth to assist and to fill many differing roles. We each struggle with some aspect of our individual separateness, but it is through these differences that we learn about ourselves and others. We are cloned only in ways of the Spirit; we are individual in the gifts that we embody. The Divine Presence within us can be utilized to help comfort and inspire us, but we must summon it into action. By asking through prayer, we show a level of trust and agreement to act in concert with the response. If we express thankfulness for the opportunities to learn new ways of expanding our spiritual connections to God and each other through prayer and service, we shall find the joys that bring a sense of exhilaration, a peaceful balance to our souls, and the comfort of connection. We shall, indeed, feel fulfilled.

As we enter into daily prayer, meditation, and communion with Spirit, our needs will not go unanswered or unfulfilled. It is not *how* one prays, but *if* one prays. The answer does not rest is answering "whether or not God is available," but in believing that this unifying force exists within and works through each and every one of us. We arrived here filled with Spirit, and our souls will depart the earth plane still filled with Spirit. We all, each and every one of us, desire and need direct experience of conscious contact with the Divine.

God is life—not some life, but all life.
God is action—not some action, but all action.
God is power—not some power, but all power.
God is presence—not some presence, but all presence.

LIGHTING YOUR SPIRITUAL PASSION

God is pure Spirit, filling all space. This pure Spirit animates our every act. There is a real you, which lives in a real God, and a physical you. The two are one. To realize and know this is to understand the secret of life. To realize this is to understand that you have a relationship with the Divine Presence. To realize that the law of God is written in your own mind is to make available to you a power that can meet every need—including the need for connection. (Ernst Holmes)

Ultimately, it is not *how* one prays, but *if* one prays. The Divine Presence can offer both intervention and comfort, but only when we believe it exists and is available to each of us.

CHAPTER 7

The Circle

Chapter 7

The Circle

We often hear about "the circle of life," and Native Americans talk about "the medicine wheel" as being symbolic of our life process. Even our minds can be seen as a circle with corridors that lead out into the four directions:

- East is the mental
- West is the physical
- North is the spiritual
- South is the emotional

As we travel our path, we often come to steps that can be thought of as progressions in our levels of awareness. We climb the steps of learning as we explore the mystery into which we all are born. As we walk through veils of uncertainty, we gradually move up the spiraling circle of progress into higher levels of vibration. Each progressive ascent brings us closer to Spirit, closer to the essence of our birth. The yearning to find that which birthed our very soul eventually brings us back, full circle, to the very core energy from which we were created.

Our imagination allows us the freedom to roam internally through the circle of our minds. As we explore all four directions, we can invite Spirit into this, our inner circle, into the

LIGHTING YOUR SPIRITUAL PASSION

Being that is Self. In doing so, we offer our soul back to that from which we came. We are, in truth, offering to sacrifice our ego for a few moments, to lay the ego aside and allow God to fill us with the abundance of direct contact, which is grace. We often call this time meditation or prayer.

As we travel the four directions into the physical, mental, emotional, and spiritual arenas, we are setting the internal foundation for the circling energy to spiral upward as it expands. When heat fills a container, it searches for upward space to expand. The same idea is present in all spiritual work. The physical body actually warms when it contacts Spirit because it is excited, and this excitement raises the vibrations. We can sense accelerated vibration, often manifesting as goose bumps, as we offer our soul back to that from which we came.

For North American indigenous peoples, reaching the center of the medicine wheel is similar to mountain climbers reaching the peak of the mountain, the center of the apex of the physical mass that rises above the floor of the earth. By connecting with that particular peak or the center of the medicine wheel, one feels sacred, feels divine, feels closer to God.

Envisioning a circle of light in your mind's eye (your imagination) is a beautiful way to center the body and the mind. This light can be any color that you need/want at the moment, and you can spiral it upward. As you offer yourself up for spiritual connection, you rise into higher levels of consciousness. Once you achieve this feeling, you are beginning to experience transformational potential, which is life's natural direction. Life wants to exist, to go on, and it yearns to expand in awareness.

We are curious, and we have been given the magnificent gift of free choice. We can choose to pursue a spiritual path or

The Circle

we can choose to believe that this material existence on earth is, simply, all there is and will ever be. The choice is ours. Sometimes this gift of choice is almost too much for us because the opportunities to use our free choice can often feel burdensome. We sometimes labor under the yoke of freedom of choice, not knowing which direction to turn without someone else to guide us. Sometimes we simply keep moving around the circle of life in repetitive paths without spiraling upward in our spiritual awareness…we feel stuck.

But we are the vehicle for free choice to manifest LOVE here on Earth. We are the Hands of God on Earth, and it is our challenge and our opportunity to use the freedom of choice to improve the way life functions on Earth. We are the way that life can go on, and we can magnify our connections back to the spiritual realm by offering to be the vehicle that can transform the burden of free choice. It is in accepting the responsibilities that we bring transformation into the equation. We can, by offering ourselves back to God, come full circle with the LOVE from which we were born. Guidance and support is always available from the spiritual realm, the source of our strength.

When we feel called to respond to a new idea, spiraling spiritual energy begins to lift us from where we are now to where we are going to be next. Once we are exposed to new ideas, the encounters can lead us into new levels of awareness, resulting in new ways of being in the world. We get bored because we are ready for the next level, because we want to move around the circle of awareness again; we want to be lifted higher. This elevated feeling can come temporarily from being entertained, or it can come with greater permanence from deep internal work that teaches us more about the truth

LIGHTING YOUR SPIRITUAL PASSION

of life. Life wants to experience itself through us; life wants to expand in awareness.

These spiritual experiences of relief from boredom through "upliftment" and enlightenment remain embedded in our soul's memory, and we yearn to keep moving around and up. We are altered through opening ourselves to Spirit We become a provider of more life experience rather than just existing as a consumer of life. We are constantly being propelled around the wheel of spiraling energy because everything is constantly in motion. Life rarely sits still for very long. Change is a constant experience. This is what we mean when we talk about the process of spiritual growth AS the goal. We are never going to arrive at the end of our work, because our work is to evolve into whatever is next for us spiritually. It is the process of transformation that brings our experiences of grace.

Our spiritual hunger is something to be welcomed; it is a gift. We continue to search for knowledge, truth, and enlightenment so that we can continue to search for knowledge, truth, and enlightenment. We walk on the skin of Mother Earth, we drink from her rivers of knowledge, we share her sun, moon, and stars as we engage in life on this small circular ball floating in the universe. We are walking forward into our past as we stay on the path that leads us from here into our future levels of awareness until we travel full circle, back into that Spirit from which we were born.

The circle exemplifies the unending process of internal exploration and unfolding that leads to deeper spiritual awareness and wisdom. Perhaps you might want to have a circle symbol in full view in your home to remind you that goals in life are simply benchmarks along your upward-spiraling journey.

CHAPTER 8

The Power of Forgiveness

Chapter 8

The Power of Forgiveness

It is our individual personalities that determine who we are and how we are perceived by others. Our personalities are intertwined with astrology, numerology, body form, hair and skin colors, and a myriad of identifiers and experiences that have molded us into who we are today. Our spiritual beliefs and the ongoing expansion of our spiritual awareness are also important components in determining who we are and how we live in this world. And all of the above contribute to how we make decisions and how we relate to others.

Are your decisions conscious or are they knee-jerk reactions? When confronted with adversity, how do you choose to relate to the problem? Do you allow yourself time to think before responding when you feel defensive or challenged? Do you contemplate just how your responses might affect others as well as yourself? Traveling the road of life, we must face these questions so that we can handle difficult situations with an understanding that "win-win" results are always possible. It is in the exploration of difficulties that we often find common ground. We call the process mediation, and the results are usually a compromise; mediation grows equality while eliminating

LIGHTING YOUR SPIRITUAL PASSION

winners and losers. Our spiritual foundation is often revealed in our responses to adversity.

Do you give people plenty of space to express their feelings and opinions? How often is it important to you to "be right"? How often does someone "rub you the wrong way"? How often do you critique others' actions? And how do you move from a position of critical judgment to one of mediation and acceptance? What is the process that you use to question your own motives and actions? In your past experiences, did both sides lose? How could both sides have experienced more equal footing? Did you ask the other side what was the most important consideration to them at that time? Are you willing to budge so that a compromise can be reached? Is forgiveness an easy process for you to move through, or is it lengthy and painful?

Sometimes problematic situations arise because we do not like another's behavior and feel a need to speak up about it. Perhaps we feel that person is headed in a direction that is not in their best interest. It is often difficult to accept another's decision when that decision feels "wrong" to us. Just because we allow another the space to make a decision does not mean that we are supporting the decision. There is a significant difference between telling someone that you think they are making the right decision and supporting them through their decision process—no matter what they eventually choose. Unconditional love is about supporting, not about agreeing with others' decisions. There is a difference. You might wish that a friend was not filing for divorce, overspending their budget, leaving a stable job, or fighting with someone, but those choices are theirs.

The Power of Forgiveness

When we disagree with another's choice, we can listen, care, express our opinion, be patient with what might appear to us as rationalizations, and watch with compassion as events unfold. We might not agree with their path, but we still have the opportunity to express unconditional love and to learn from the experience of loving unconditionally.

I believe that unconditional love really sets our internal stage for forgiveness. Once we understand that every individual has a right to choose their own experiences and their personal responses to those experiences, we understand much more about living an authentic life. An authentic life usually involves taking risks. Risks, even the most carefully calculated, involve error and disappointment. And forgiveness is a key ingredient. While those who never dare to risk also never feel the sheer exhilaration of personal success, they also must learn how to forgive both themselves and others—when the risk doesn't produce the desired result—in order to continue moving forward in life. Accepting the fact that we will make mistakes, and that we will need to offer forgiveness, expands our spirituality. Acceptance is foundational for both unconditional love and forgiveness.

Perhaps the learning that occurs from these processes is much more important than the outcome. Can we accept that premise in the very beginning stages and be compassionate? And where do we draw the line regarding the amount of time and energy and personal involvement? How we answer becomes our part of the unconditional love equation. The Great Spirit experiences how we use the free will that is our birthright; will we offer to forgive when wounded? Have we learned that holding a grudge hurts the one who clings to it? Forgiveness frees both sides of a conflict.

LIGHTING YOUR SPIRITUAL PASSION

What if the experience of feeling betrayed or hurt is truly the gift in dealing with difficulty? And what if we are drawn into such a situation because the unfolding process of forgiveness benefits both sides in some unforeseen way from the very beginning of the situation? These questions and the resulting answers can offer us expanded views of conflict and difficulty. We often hear that in every problem is an opportunity; maybe this is really true! Living through the process of conflict and resolution is not easy, but it is educational if we pay attention and learn from our interactions with each other. When emotions flare, love often takes a backseat.

And often it is one group of people arguing with another group—sometimes even within our churches, where people might feel empowered by the sheer numbers involved. But we also have to remember the increased potential for damage when negative energy is shared and fed. What happens when there is disagreement within a place that so many come to for comfort and emotional safety? How do we support each other's individual paths within a church community when competition arises? How often do power issues split churches into two (or more) smaller fragments in the very place that we came searching for unity?

It is in finding the common threads keeping us tied to each other that we weave a stronger fabric of spiritual unity. The threads are unconditional love, compassion, and forgiveness. The fabric is the knowing that we have all come from and are going back to that which created us. I view this fabric as bright and multicolored, with the essence of every person making a vibrant contribution.

This is the true challenge: how to have a supportive, active community that meets the needs of its people. This is the true

The Power of Forgiveness

challenge throughout the world, and a real test of issues relating to greed, power, and dominance. Anger, disagreement, and splintered relationships leave many feeling disappointed and abandoned in places where they came seeking solace. Fear feeds the personality fires, and people can be left feeling charred— emotionally burned and damaged. This is when some friendships, marriages, families, churches, and communities split – and both sides are then required to rebuild. Fear destroys and trust builds.

Acceptance grows into unconditional love, the foundation for forgiveness. Forgiveness frees us from the cage of judgment and narrow-mindedness and expands our capacity to both give and receive unconditional love.

Let us all remember that we can take the time to listen, to treat each other with dignity and respect. We get back what we give out; it is about the natural law of attraction. We are living, breathing, physical organisms with the power of choice to hold grudges or to forgive. We can remember past injustices and cling to them like a security blanket, or we can look forward to working together and plan how to make compromise more plausible in our daily lives. We can live from a position of self-protection and fear, and remain in the status quo, or we can live from a position of unconditional love and trust and evolve into something truly beyond our imagination. Which path do you choose?

CHAPTER 9

Finding God at the Beach

Chapter 9

Finding God at the Beach

This late spring morning, after spending nine months in the Arizona desert, I returned to Maine's magnificent Penobscot Bay. The sun was low on the dawn's horizon, and gentle waves lapped the shoreline in welcome. Lobster boats bobbed in the harbor, and one lone sailboat crept silently around Sears Island. I walked out onto the coarse sand bar, listening as my footsteps echoed back, back, back to former times when I came here to rid myself of stress and pain after 60- to 70-hour workweeks. Today the lapping waves felt like gentle kisses on my toes.

Church had been on my mind when I'd woken up this morning—but there was no church service today. I had simply wanted to be with Spirit, so I'd driven four miles from my house to my favorite sea glass–collecting spot. And there it was—silent and peaceful. No other person was in sight. Ah! I could have a blessed solitary low-tide walk out to the far reaches of the ocean's floor, where few ever trod.

When the earth is experiencing a full moon, the tides retreat to unusually low levels, revealing previously hidden treasures. Arriving at the waterline, I stopped. I could smell

LIGHTING YOUR SPIRITUAL PASSION

the fresh rockweed, now exposed by the retreating tide, as it began to steam in the early morning's direct sun rays. Rockweed pods began to audibly *pop, pop, pop* as they dried and their skins cracked open. The sounds seemed like little expressions of joy! It was truly a fairy-tale land of mist and ocean and sun. Even the seagulls sat silently on the rocks, waiting...just being present.

I had wanted a church service, and here it was. Nature was ablaze with her glorious slant of light on the water and in the scent of steaming rockweed as the sun's rays released pops of moisture into the air. Dampness filled my lungs and my soul; I was spiritually refreshed. Spirit replenished my awe and my adoration of Nature's amazing glories. Today, my personal church service was celebrated at the ocean's edge; I went looking for sea glass, and I found God.

Places designated as spiritual are often where we materially focused humans go to find God. But my life has taught me that I find spiritual connections and internal balance out in nature rather than in a human-made sanctuary. God is often discovered smack in the midst of natural beauty.

CHAPTER 10

Clearing Clutter = Making Space for Spirit

Chapter 10

Clearing Clutter = Making Space for Spirit

Even though I'm a person who enjoys being involved in a lot of different projects, it took me quite a long time to understand that clutter in any form creates even more chaos. One day, I was reading and came across a chapter about cleaning out the attic of the mind. The author stressed that when we live surrounded by clutter, our mind's ability to organize thoughts and our spiritual growth are both thwarted. The clutter symbolizes the lack of internal organization and functioning abilities in our lives. If we begin to clean out—to sort and discard—our physical space, then we are beginning to prioritize what is really important. The very process of sorting through our clutter, making choices about what to keep and what to discard, clears the cobwebs out of our mind. We begin to focus on what is truly important. The physical cleaning is reflected in the mental organization of prioritizing.

When our lives are already crammed full of activities, material possessions, and things that we believe we "should" attend to, the freedom to flow in tandem with Spirit is sorely

LIGHTING YOUR SPIRITUAL PASSION

inhibited. That is why, as we evolve spiritually, we often discover that material possessions actually weigh us down.

Try removing everything from one cluttered area in your personal living space and then only put in full sight what you want to be reminded of every single day. What objects would you place there to help you function at the optimum level? The remaining items can be put into boxes, closets, filing cabinets, drawers, or wherever you choose, or you can donate them to a charity or have a yard sale. You are making room for the *new* to enter your life. Keep what feels significant and put away, out of sight, what you no longer choose to view (or trip over) every day. Discard what no longer serves you.

There is a great internal power and strength that rises up during this physical cleaning and sorting out process. Actually digging in, sorting, and cleaning out our physical space also gives our brain a cleaner slate. It is almost as if your mind is saying, "Oh, we are no longer going to have disinterest, confusion, and disorganization as our visual landscape every day. Now we are going to have the semblance of clarity about what is important to mold our personal living space."

Just as when you empty out a room, you create an open space in your mind. Some of you probably already create this open space in your daily meditations or prayers, and then you simply observe what arises. In order to receive new information, there must be both a summoning and a place for the information to rest while you examine it.

We all know the feeling of having company and going through the rushed process of hiding our clutter, dusting and cleaning off the furniture, changing the beds, and sorting through old mail and papers. When we are finished, all looks

Clearing Clutter = Making Space for Spirit

pretty good! We then wonder why we allowed junk to accumulate. When clutter rules your personal living space, you crowd out spiritual connections. When you organize your space and your time, and monitor your thoughts to allow only that which is positive and productive, you move forward into a much higher realm of functioning in the world. It is the ongoing process of discernment, of internal monitoring, that frees us to move closer to Spirit.

Creating *space* for Spirit to enter is a key part of keeping our thoughts *open* to Spirit. Opening fresh spaces invites new ways of viewing old problems. Throwing out negative emotions or old "hurts" as if they were trash (which they are), leaves us ready to receive more positive experiences. We feel refreshed, cleansed, and ready to welcome the "new." We feel that we have lightened our daily load.

Remember the Old Testament verse that admonishes us to "set thine house in order"? Order has value; its very definition includes references to a state of being peaceful. Peace certainly invites Spirit. If clutter creates confusion, does order create peacefulness? I think so.

Have you moved to a new location recently? Moving certainly requires cleaning out and organizing, usually a tremendous amount of effort spread over many weeks. But once the dust has settled and we are firmly planted in a new location, many of the boxes that we thought we had to bring to the new house often remain unpacked in the garage, attic, or basement for years. We cling to the memories of how those material possessions served us in the past—but maybe they are not relevant to our current life. Maybe those books that are two decades old remind you of when Spirit was not a part of your daily routine.

LIGHTING YOUR SPIRITUAL PASSION

Maybe those clothes no longer fit you and someone else could use them. Do those physical items hold memories and clutter your thoughts?

Our relationship with things is often a mirror for our relationship with God and the spirits of those who have gone before us. When we lose a loved one, cleaning out their possessions is one way of being able to be with them over and over and over again. While this can bring up painful feelings of loss, the process also renews happy memories and allows us the experience of being close. When we leave their clothes in a closet for years, or don't change anything in their bedroom, or refuse to discard any of their possessions, we are locking ourselves into a state of internal clutter by refusing to live in the present. The grief process involves sorting through memories as we move from the past into the present, deciding which ones you want to keep in your heart and which ones you are better off letting go.

Many of us were raised by Depression-trained parents; therefore we became hoarders of anything that we might need "someday." Have we mentally hoarded thoughts and feelings that we might use someday? We all know what that feels like—to hang on desperately to that which no longer serves us. It is like dancing with ghosts to music that is no longer playing! Our minds and spirits can become so filled with useless clutter—so cluttered that clear information cannot filter through. We yearn to be an open channel; we can provide wider and more brightly illuminated pathways.

If we make an effort to put things away rather than just dropping them on a desk or table or floor, we have a better view of our personal space. As an example, before setting the daily mail on

Clearing Clutter = Making Space for Spirit

the table, sorting out and throwing away the junk mail enables us to see the important letters and bills. Then open the remaining envelopes and throw them away, saving just the important contents. Immediately opening the remaining mail and discarding the envelopes and irrelevant enclosures allows us to focus on the important contents. Our mail is just one simple example. Having a clear vista means that we do not block our energy paths and we can feel freer to be led forward into experiences with deeper and deeper spiritual connections. We also have visual space to perceive a slant of light, a shadow, or a form. Perhaps spirit beings have been trying to get your attention...open your receptivity!

Your personal space is a direct reflection of your internal space. It is also a reflection of how you really want to portray yourself to the world. If you are living amidst much clutter, you probably are wandering around in an internal mess also. Keeping things organized around you actually increases your productivity while reducing stress and preventing burnout. Being able to find what you need when you want it is similar to being able to access Spirit whenever you feel the need. Being organized allows you to dream bigger dreams and to implement effective strategies for their realization. Remember Robin Steger's famous phrase: "Planning is as natural to the process of success as its absence is to the process of failure."

Less is actually more. You can do more if you carry less along on your life journey. I have always believed that a deeply committed spiritual path does not run through rooms filled with clutter. Clutter reflects confusion—a lack of being clear. Do not allow disorder and mayhem to have a place in your home. Each day, spend just a few minutes honoring your spiritual self by orienting your home toward order.

LIGHTING YOUR SPIRITUAL PASSION

It is important that we honor sacred space and time within our homes every single day. How do you see, hear, feel, taste, and smell spiritual energy? Is the overabundance of stuff in your space creating blockages? If you can't feel spiritual energy moving through your physical living space, how can you expect to feel it moving through your mental living space? Infinite Intelligence offers us unlimited opportunities to evolve into profoundly resonant ways of knowing—but we must clear out the clutter so that we can perceive the Light.

Spirit thrives on invitation, but in order to feel welcome it needs to have a place to roost in your heart. Consider making a list of what is cluttering up your life—both internally and externally—and then move into action. Each step that we take toward an organized life is a step toward closer communion with Spirit. If we organize our space to reflect who we truly are—magnificent messengers doing the work of Infinite Intelligence right here on earth, every day of our lives—we organize our mental space to do the same.

CHAPTER 11

Moving Forward into Center

Chapter 11

Moving Forward into Center

Spiritual work stresses personal responsibility. As people who enjoy the freedom to practice our chosen beliefs, we have a responsibility to be involved in our country's political process. As spiritually based humans, we have a responsibility to work toward promoting peace. When we are actively engaged in participating, we can be part of making a difference in the future of the world. Helping to shift the political process from fear-based aggression to trust-based cooperation is important, and if we keep reminders front and center, we can contribute to making a difference. *In*difference has never solved any problems.

Some religious movements believe that if the world would just follow their accepted tenets all would be right. This attitude sets up conflict between religious systems, and we end up exactly where we have always been—enmeshed in seemingly irresolvable differences. We see similar situations between countries. And we observe science and religion, often described as being at opposite poles, moving forward around the circle of awareness. In recent years, we hear more about the agreements, and less about the differences, between science and religion.

LIGHTING YOUR SPIRITUAL PASSION

For example, medical physician Dr. Raymond Moody has written fascinating stories told by Near Death Experience survivors about where their consciousness traveled when they were clinically dead. He put his successful medical career on the line by publishing tales of NDE's with amazingly similar details. Science has repeatedly denied that there has been any proof of an afterlife, but when Dr. Moody began speaking out, so did other physicians. Science and religion are offering a glimpse of forward movement into a more peaceful coexistence. This is the vision that we can embrace and share among our political parties and all peoples, in all countries, upon planet Earth.

When we are able to mediate an agreement benefiting all sides, there is a deep feeling of cooperation and respect. However, if we continue to pursue a desire to win, everyone ends up losing. Power struggles never result in victory. Power struggles result in inequality. Everything on our planet works at optimum efficiency when there is respect for the flourishing of all life; only then do we have sustainable coexistence.

Let us always remember that we are conscious agents in our own evolutionary development. If you feel as though your voice doesn't really make any difference, maybe it is because you have been silent. Is it time to add your voice to the cares and concerns of the world where we are so privileged to live? Is it time for you to contribute an idea for a peaceful solution to a problem in your home, church, community, state, country, or world? Maybe, just maybe, your idea is the solution. Problems are solved one step at a time with one person at a time. You might be just the person needed to bring a solution to something that has troubled you. Step forward and become involved; become God's hands on Earth.

Moving Forward into Center

As we move through this politically vibrant time in our history when we can exercise our gift of living in a free democracy, let us remember that humans have exhibited tremendous potential for violence and aggression. We have an opportunity each day to speak up by mail, e-mail, telephone, or in person to make the world a tiny bit better. Even little things can make a big difference, because little acts contribute energetically to a bigger shift. We have the chance to make a difference, to bend the energy toward involved concern and caring. As rational, thinking individuals, we must remind ourselves that we are not helpless. In fact, we are truly powerful beyond measure. Believe this and move into action.

It is very exciting that science has discovered that energy is all there is. This discovery is really profound, and it relates to everything that we know as real. If matter is composed simply of energy, and if our soul's path is about movement, then there is certainly hope that our conditioned response of declaring war on everything that we disagree with might be transformed. Rather than having a mentality aimed toward winning, perhaps we can have an evolution of human mentality that is about nurturing and sustaining. This evolution in thinking is showing itself with increased awareness of damage to our planet and with the United Nations' efforts in understanding that people need clean water, unpolluted earth to grow food, and shelter from the elements. Without these fundamental needs being met, there will continue to be attitudes of "You have it, I don't, and I am coming to take it away from you." We call it war, but it is really about fear and inequality. Our coexistence is not (and never has been) about winning; coexistence is about cooperation and learning to work together

LIGHTING YOUR SPIRITUAL PASSION

by attempting to understand another's viewpoint—whatever the issue might be. There is always common ground.

We know the peace that comes from connecting with Spirit, and we know that this experience of peace is always available to us. When we forget about the availability of peace, when this knowledge is undermined by some sense of fear, we move into the mode of aggression. Experiencing peace encourages more healthy growth; experiencing fear inhibits healthy forward progress. Once again we come back to the element of trust. When we trust, there is no fear, and then peace is possible. We must remember to trust in the indwelling presence of God and that spiritual guidance is available and accessible when we ask for it. Trust opens the door to a better future for all.

Trust means not looking back over our shoulders at "how we have been wronged." Trust is about looking forward into ways that we can use to merge more deeply with all that is, moving forward into center, resulting in a higher evolutionary process of movement into peace. When there is an experience of deep connectedness and belonging, this works like a magnet attracting us back to the Source, and it magnifies the Light of Love as it draws more and more individuals to it. This is what peace work is all about: attracting more and more individuals into the fold of inter-connectedness.

Science is rational and mind-based; spirituality is innate and soul-based. It is in the blending of these two qualities that we shall come into full-circle awareness, leading to an understanding of the mission of peace. Are we hard-wired for peace? (Some say we are hard-wired for war, but I do not believe that's true.) When we trust, like an infant, we will grab onto any hand that reaches out to us. We do not come into the world filled

Moving Forward into Center

with fear and self-protection. We want to be connected—we love to be held, to hug, to laugh, and to simply be with others. We need to know that comfort can be found and our needs can be met. There is always a peaceful resolution available. We have to find it.

Fear is learned; let us be very careful in what we are teaching our young people about lack of trust. Yes, we do have to live in today's world, but if we each model trust and acceptance, it will bloom and spread. Perhaps we are not hard-wired for peace or fear, but are hard-wired with the amazing responsibility of choice. We can choose which mode of operation we want to exhibit in the world.

I remember reading about an interview with the Dalai Lama. He was describing an ancient Buddhist meditation technique that involves sitting in silence and feeling the self completely filled with a love that is supportive, kind, and warm in every way. Then the Buddhist directs this feeling of total love out to others. It is easy to send loving thoughts to those we already love, but the intent here is to include those whom you feel neutral about, and then move on to those whom you really do not feel drawn to love. This meditation is about opening the heart through an act of kindness and giving. We can train ourselves to be more loving by having loving thoughts and by acting in loving ways. Just imagine the joy that this could bring into our daily lives!

If you think that you are too small to make a difference in the world, you might want to remember the experience of being in bed with a mosquito! You are only as small as you think you are. Peace can only be as important in the world as we choose to make it. If it is important to you, then propel it

LIGHTING YOUR SPIRITUAL PASSION

forward into the center of your being. In turn, this will help bring a peaceful center into the world. Each of us must start with the self, which then can begin to serve as a mentor for others. The world is hungry for peace, the earth needs it to heal, and humanity (and all life on this planet) needs it to survive.

CHAPTER 12

Opening into Spirit

Chapter 12

Opening into Spirit

Nature is a profound reminder of the abundance and beauty of our life process here on earth. The importance of recognizing the beauty of Spirit—in scent, vision, taste, smell, and touch—is brought back into our awareness over and over again. But each one of us is personally responsible for noticing these opportunities. Nature becomes a window into spiritual magnificence, allowing for an inner opening into Spirit. Are humans, with our densely conditioned minds, ready for a transformation of consciousness into deeper spiritual awareness? Are we ready to move into a global philosophy of unity and caring for all? We are the hands of God; we possess the capacity to heal the Earth.

Our world has been, for the most part, led by egotistic personalities. Each leader has been out to make a name for himself, using the guise of "protecting the people" as a verbal defense for waging conflict. So we now have centuries upon centuries of egos fighting against egos—and no one ever really "wins." We cannot fight against the ego and win.

Is the light of consciousness expanding throughout our world? I think it is, and I believe that each one of us is a spark

LIGHTING YOUR SPIRITUAL PASSION

of that light. We are the light that will bring forward change; we are the Voice of Infinite Intelligence on Earth. Spiritually based persons know the joy that comes from spreading light, eliminating fear, and inspiring trust through enlightened awareness. Our world is hungry for light, and we can feed that hunger. Our Earth has been plundered and raped, animals have been hunted to extinction, and there is pervasive inequality based on gender, skin color, nationality, and religion.

Eckhart Tolle's popular book, *A New Earth*, states that the radical transformation of human consciousness is called enlightenment, which would be the greatest achievement of humanity. Recognizing our own ego-based insanity, which has thrived on a mindset of "us against them," is the beginning of healing and transcendence. Our cultures took some of the greatest teachings of the most enlightened spiritual leaders and distorted these teachings to make them self-serving. But these religions share a core truth—*the* Truth: we are all interconnected. Everything on Earth has come out of Spirit, and we are all interdependent. Ancient cultures, including Native Americans, believed in the indwelling Spirit in everything. This is the Truth and we have chosen to ignore it.

The history of our planetary behavior, in hindsight, looks reprehensible. Rather than admiring and learning about magnificent animals like gorillas, tigers, and elephants, we have sought to kill and destroy them for trophies. Poachers "harvest" these magnificent creatures and sell animals' body parts. We have encroached and destroyed many animals' habitats. Others, such as wolves, have been reduced to dangerously low numbers by extermination because they endangered livestock or were too close to human populations.

Opening into Spirit

What have we been thinking? Where has this repetitive divide-and-conquer mindset brought us? Do we really believe that we can eradicate populations that we deem to be "invasive" without damaging ourselves? How difficult is it to understand that we are all interconnected and that our survival depends on the survival of all species? These old ego-based patterns, which eventually lead to self-destruction, have brought us to a critical time on our planet. We have damaged and destroyed the very land, air, and water that are imperative to survival for all. We have misplaced the sense of sacredness in nature; we thought (perhaps subconsciously) that we could manipulate, damage, and destroy Earth's magnificence with no lasting effect on humans. We were wrong.

The expanding knowledge of our interconnectedness, leading us deeper into spiritual awareness, is the only thing that can save the Earth and all of its inhabitants. Living in the "now" and using what you have, and not what you hope to buy in the future, is about conscious presence. The Truth is comprised of respect for all and being grateful for the gift of life.

Learning to be a beacon of respect, interconnectedness, and gratitude comes from making conscious decisions about our behaviors. In our society, greed is rewarded as we amass and compare our possessions. To step out of this rut, we must remind ourselves—every single day—that we choose to walk a spiritually based path toward enlightenment. We choose to be grateful, and we choose to remember that all abundance comes from the Source of our Being. As we examine the people and things we are emotionally attached to, we must become aware of how we prioritize our attachments; Tolle says that this is the

LIGHTING YOUR SPIRITUAL PASSION

beginning of the transformation of consciousness, which will happen one person at a time. The move toward enlightened awareness is a long and necessary process into unity.

This transformation of consciousness leads to more compassion, more understanding. It also leads into deeper wisdom and the experience of feeling more love. That sense of companionship, of a Presence that is always available, eliminates fear and brings more peacefulness into our lives. It helps us to live in the present with a sense of expanded openness for what simply *is*. Resistance, which sets up rigidity internally, begins to dissolve and we flow with the warmth of spiritual awareness. We operate more and more from a position of connection rather than separation. And we recognize that keeping things honest helps to eliminate emotionality in our daily lives as we become simply more accepting of the "now." The wise sage part of us begins to emerge, and we become less and less needy.

There are many paths into the Light of awareness. Choose a path that resonates deep inside of you—a path that you believe you can honor and walk. Natural Laws state that whatever we choose to remain focused on actually becomes our reality as we attract more and more of that into our lives. So it seems wise to choose respect and gratitude as a focal point for our daily practice, doesn't it? Respect and gratitude involve "bearing witness" to our own thoughts and behaviors. We must each be our own internal observer as we strive to live within the present moment.

What thoughts, behaviors, and beliefs do you choose to embrace within your mind and body? Whatever you choose, that is what you are strengthening with each thought and action. Bearing witness to self is the key that unlocks the door

Opening into Spirit

into deeper levels of peace and happiness because you are understanding and accepting yourself. You are no longer living from others' expectations of what you "should" be; you are becoming comfortable within your own skin.

As human consciousness evolves, through committed intentions to honor our interconnectedness, our planet will begin to heal. Animals will glean more respect as we understand more about the delicate balance of Nature and how each part is dependent on all other parts. Relations between countries will soften. Cooperative interaction will lead us into deeper levels of awareness. We can grow into the wisdom of unity consciousness. The potential for magnificence is not out there...somewhere; the potential for magnificence is here right now—inside each and every one of us!

When we learn to give, we can then receive. We cannot receive what we don't give. If you feel that you have everything you need, you will attract more abundance into your life. But if you always feel a lack, if you perceive your life as unfulfilled and empty, then you will attract more scarcity into your arena. The opposite of scarcity is "enough." Which would you prefer?

For me, Nature is the key to being in the present. Nature expresses the glorious abundance of creation, and when we connect with Nature at a spiritual level, we are connecting with abundance. I choose to have more abundant experiences; those experiences can be magnetically attracted into my personal space when I feel grateful for the chance to sit by a rushing stream, to observe a colorful sunset, or to walk in the ocean's lapping waves along the shoreline. When I merge with Nature, I am both giving (gratitude) and receiving (spiritual rejuvenation).

LIGHTING YOUR SPIRITUAL PASSION

Nature is sacred; Nature is perfect. It does not need weeding. Nature does not need improvement. Nature is perfect, and connecting with that perfection brings peace, joy and inner happiness because we are then in touch with Infinite Intelligence at a conscious level. When we are in the present, fully immersed in Nature, the ego shrinks. The sense of time diminishes and we are imbued with Spirit. Ah! This is when we can create, when we are at our optimum level to receive. This is when happiness abounds in every cell in our body as it is released from the ego's imprisonment. Nature nurtures the soul.

In the stillness of merging with Nature, you will hear and know God. Nature is the window to spiritual connection. In Nature, you will experience grace, and out of that experience will come desire. You will desire to be of service, to bring more Light consciousness into the world, and, in turn, you will desire to experience more grace. Feed your hungry soul with the bounty of Nature, which will always have the power to fill you when you feel spiritually empty. Nature inspires a quickening in the soul.

Your process of enlightenment will be initiated. It is a thrilling experience. You will become less resistant, more open. You will become less judgmental, more accepting. And you will experience less attachment to things and situations—you will *allow* yourself to be lead into deeper spiritual connections. Once the window to spiritual connectivity has been cracked open, you will be different. As a channel for bringing more Light into our world, your inner purpose and outer purpose will merge into one presence. You will become a field of awareness for yourself and others, and you will know your purpose on Earth. Expansion of consciousness alters you, and your

Opening into Spirit

changes affect others. The old ways of wanting and fearing—emotions that left you feeling unhappy and unfulfilled—will gradually dissipate because they no longer serve you. You will be filled with trust, understanding about when to wait, and love for all.

Yes, the future is unknown, but the fear that used to push opportunities away will be gone. You will step into the magnificent mystery of life, and anything that you desire will become possible. Tolle says that when uncertainty is acceptable, you have increased aliveness, alertness, and creativity. When you *allow*, synchronicity becomes common as stress subsides. You will enjoy increased energy levels as you move forward into deeper spiritual awareness because you will operate from a position of connected acceptance rather than separated resistance. You will feel the joy of life's pulsing, magnetic energy drawing you closer and closer to God. Your enthusiasm will fuel your efforts and will inspire others with your aliveness and vitality. As you live from a position of inclusive connectedness, you will experience abundance as you manifest what you give.

Many of the ideas in this chapter are based on concepts from Eckhart Tolle's book, *A New Earth* (Penguin Group, 2005).

CHAPTER 13

Honoring Completion

Chapter 13

Honoring Completion

The month of May, which includes both Mother's Day and Memorial Day, is about coming full circle. Becoming a mother is about giving birth into physical form; memorializing those who have transitioned is about honoring those who have been birthed into spiritual form. Both of these holidays honor the process of coming full circle through life.

Our mothers cared for our physical well-being as they carried us, nestled deep in their wombs, for nine months of gestation. Then they cradled us in their physical arms of love. They molded our personalities as they guided us through years of childhood; they kept us safe and taught us how to walk our own path. Mothers are our primary source of everything that we know and experience about life because we were formed out of the very fabric of their bodies. As we entered the birth canal, eventually taking our first breath, our mothers' voices were the core of everything familiar for us. Fathers also have a vital role in rearing children, but we grow into readiness for life inside of the mother. Her heartbeat, her voice, her movements, her rhythm of walking, her eating habits, and eventually her touch and her scent are what we first know.

LIGHTING YOUR SPIRITUAL PASSION

And while we honor all mothers on Mother's Day, we also remember that we were the greatest gift and the greatest joy—during pregnancy and birth—that our mothers have probably ever known. Mothering, while filled with the most joyous experiences, can also embrace some of the very deepest pain. When a woman gives birth to a baby, part of the mother goes out into the world with the child. That is a mother's legacy: that, through her children, she will continue to live on earth long after she has transitioned to spirit form.

When the child precedes her in death, part of the mother also goes with the child's spirit. On Memorial Day, which was created to honor those fallen in war, we also remember all of those children who have left earth earlier than we expected, and we remember the mothers who have gone through the trauma of losing a child. These women, throughout the rest of their earthly lives, need our love and support. We remember all parents who have grieved for the loss of future time with their beloved children.

Also on Memorial Day, we remember our feelings as we attended memorial services and funerals, and examined the seeming emptiness of our lives when loved ones transitioned. We remember those who openly shared their love with us and allowed us to love them back wholeheartedly.

As we look back, we are acutely attuned to our loved ones' continuing existence in another realm. We know that they are with us and that they continue to feel the love that we send to them. On Memorial Day, we honor them while remembering their physical passing. They transitioned from earthly form through death, birthing into the realm of Spirit.

Coming full circle was really brought home to me recently when my father transitioned on his 89th birthday. His room

Honoring Completion

was filled with "Happy Birthday, Ed" balloons when he took his final breath. His peaceful countenance belied his long lifespan. He transitioned from being an elderly, frail, often confused man who hated to be alone, into a state of blissfully peaceful relaxation and contentment. His face was smooth, unlined, and almost youthful as we waited for the mortuary vehicle to arrive. Sitting with him that day for twelve hours, the only experience of death was the shutting down of his physical body. Watching as his soul made its transition, I was mesmerized by his face. He looked so young! Smooth-skinned, transparent and trusting, he was on his way, being birthed into a new realm.

During the last few weeks of Dad's earthly life, he had mentioned that his father had been in to see him. (His father had transitioned some three decades earlier.) I simply replied by asking if his mother had also come to visit. "No, Father came alone," he said each time. I asked if his grandmother had visited, and I got the same answer: "No, just Father." I'm not sure why only his father had appeared, but I understood that this was Dad's way of letting me know that he was aware of his impending transition to Spirit.

Dad had never voiced a belief in any supreme being or power, but I had talked with him often about my own spiritual beliefs. Our daily talks, with Dad's very hazy memory, became more and more confusing. Down to just 120 pounds on his formerly strapping 6-foot, 185-pound frame, we knew that his earthly time was closing. His mind and his body were tired, but not his soul. It yearned to be free to reconnect with loved ones who had preceded him and with Spirit out of which he had been birthed. The visitations by his own father brought him

LIGHTING YOUR SPIRITUAL PASSION

great comfort. In turn, I was comforted by the awareness of Dad's clear acceptance of these encounters. Hospice workers (who seemed like angels to me) confirmed that these occurrences are common in their work. In the midst of Dad's confusion and loss of speech, he was able to verbalize these experiences with amazing clarity as I watched him search carefully for the "right" words to use. Dad knew that I would understand and believe him.

I have included these details in this essay as a way of personalizing the feelings that we often experience on Memorial Day as we remember and honor those whom we have loved. Perhaps my personal memories will help expand some readers' trust in the continuity of the soul after death.

Each and every one of us has the opportunity to move back into our spiritual home, back into the unending folds of Spirit and LOVE. During May, we celebrate the love that our mothers shared with us and honor their efforts in birthing us into physical form. We also honor the experience of birthing into the spiritual realm, when we shed the physical body and transition back to the Light of Spirit. These two holidays not only bookend the month of May, but also celebrate the events that bookend our physical lives.

CHAPTER 14

Growing in Spiritual Unity

Chapter 14

Growing in Spiritual Unity

Being happy is fun, and most people, if asked, would probably say that they would rather be happy than unhappy. However, happiness is actually a *choice* that we make for ourselves every minute of every day. Spiritually based folks do not blame others when we are unhappy; we do not try to escape the personal responsibility of being held accountable for our own unhappiness. This is a very high expectation that is conferred on us when we enter into the community of a Spirit-based life. Accepting personal responsibility for our own happiness does not happen overnight; achieving a thorough understanding of this concept takes personal monitoring of our emotional responses over a period of time.

Everyone has days that are better than others—that is just part of being human. Sometimes we are disappointed about one thing or another, and sometimes others' disappointments get levied back against us. It really is not about what happens in our lives every day, but about our responses to those happenings. Do we treat others with respect, thereby maintaining our own personal dignity, or do we fly off the handle and blame others for displeasing us? How we respond to personal

LIGHTING YOUR SPIRITUAL PASSION

disappointments says a lot about how we choose to live and whether we choose to be happy.

Taking responsibility for our own happiness, or lack of it, means that we examine our part in every issue that brings feelings of disappointment or unhappiness. Whenever we are disappointed by others—and feel that it is important to let them know about our unhappiness—we might want to consider looking very carefully inside ourselves first. No one likes to be disappointed, but if we trust that we were doing what we thought was best for all concerned, then the situation is open for continued discussion. Happiness is a choice based on knowing what your values are and exhibiting responses that reflect and strengthen that value system.

We can choose happiness just like we can choose apathy or misery. We always have a choice about how we respond, whether we are in a one-to-one conversation or working within a group. In groups where people are trying to work together for the betterment of the organization or cause, there will be what psychologists call "norming and storming." This is a process that involves each person finding a place within the group where they feel useful. Usually this requires some personal emotional work; some people are thrilled to be working within the group while others are searching for a way to make a meaningful contribution. We all desire to feel respected and valued, supported and nurtured. Every time people work together in groups, these processes are repeated.

When you work within a group setting, do you bring happiness in the door with you? Choosing to be happy when "out in public" is magnetic to others: people enjoy being in the company of genuinely happy people. The idea that we can improve

Growing in Spiritual Unity

our lives by accepting personal responsibility for our own happiness and how we choose to share that happiness is something many people find appealing, while others just find it confusing.

The richness of mind, body, and spirit can be fostered through community. Participating in community gives us ample opportunities to assume full responsibility for our lives in all three areas. Monitoring our thoughts, structuring our beliefs, and honoring the magnificent life force in our human bodies demonstrates our gratitude to Spirit for the opportunity to live and grow in spiritual truth. We can choose to dwell on good will, not on negativity and caustic responses. We can approach difficult issues in a way that demonstrates respect for others involved. Respect for each other promotes unity, and unity makes us stronger. There is always a way to approach issues and concerns that will result in improved relations. Mediation involves respect, and embraces flexibility and vision. It is our differences that are our greatest strengths.

Every day we have an opportunity to respond to others in ways that emulate the towering strengths of Spirit. It takes personal courage to accept responsibility for being happy or unhappy; it often feels easier to place blame on others for our unhappiness. But the truth is that when we look inside to uncover our own part in our unhappiness, layers of discontent, often built up over an entire lifetime, begin to dissolve. Each time we look inside, we bring Light into our soul. With each difficult situation, when we take the time and energy to go inside, searching for a spiritual way to respond, we grow in spiritual unity and strength. Looking back, we are often amazed at how long we tried being angry at others, and how we often placed blame on others for "making us unhappy."

LIGHTING YOUR SPIRITUAL PASSION

When we take responsibility for our own part in a difficult situation, we not only move toward unity with others through common purposes and goals, but we also move from feeling fragmented and attacked to feeling totally whole and appreciated. What a gift this process unveils!

May we each be encouraged to sprout new internal roots in our soil of personal responsibility. May we be willing to take new risks in joining together with others as we extend the welcoming hands of spiritual friendship. The word "religion" means "to bind together." Accepting personal responsibility for our own happiness or unhappiness is based on our commitment to strengthening our level of spiritual awareness and responsiveness. The result will be increased happiness and a greater sense of purpose and unity. What we give, we shall receive. Be an open vessel and allow Light to flow through your body, mind, and soul, expanding your awareness of All.

CHAPTER 15

Love Is One Mind,
One Heart, One Soul

Chapter 15

Love Is One Mind, One Heart, One Soul

Love is at the very center of our being. It calls to us throughout our lives because we yearn to be enfolded in the acceptance Love brings. We search inside ourselves through education, meditation, and prayer to lead us into deeper awareness. We also search externally by experiencing the magnificence of Nature and through exploring our personal relationships with others.

Experiencing love and connection, for me, is similar to stepping outside at night and gazing into the dark velvet dome of the sky. Little twinkles of sparkling stars, which have been in the sky for millions of years, remind us that our presence here on earth is short in comparison to the concept of eternity. Searching for love in our daily lives is much like searching for symbols of meaning in the depths of the unseen. We remember that we are all part of one mind, one heart, and one soul—the unification of all.

As we imagine the deep abyss of our universe, extending millions of miles beyond our own atmosphere, we are reminded that somewhere out there, and inside each one of us

LIGHTING YOUR SPIRITUAL PASSION

and every living thing, there is an Infinite Intelligence that continues to unfold as creation evolves. Likewise, our search for love continues to offer us more and more opportunities to connect with the life force, in all of its magnificent expressions and wonderment. We are born out of the love that this magnificent Force exemplifies. The wings of love in our heart long to fly—they long to open, allowing us to soar into the bliss of experiencing love. Our search for love and our efforts be more loving also expand our creative thinking, because we know that as we give, so we receive.

The night's darkness can feel primal, reminiscent of feelings of fear or a time of loss when we could not envision a meaningful life path in our future—a time when we felt like we were walking through life in darkness. It can be unnerving to not be able to see into the unknown. But when we trust the life process, darkness can also feel exciting and filled with the promise of new adventures. Those little twinkling stars glittering in the night sky often remind me of the ever-present hope for deeply satisfying new connections of love that are just around the next corner. That love comes forward in many different ways or forms is certainly part of what we discover when we explore the mysteries of life. How shall we choose to unfold the wings of love?

> *O, the fabulous wings unused, folded in the heart!*
> —Christopher Fry

Love offers us stability, security, and peace. And if that doesn't seem to ring true for all of your love experiences, then those that don't match up are not about love. The way that

Love Is One Mind, One Heart, One Soul

we behave, one to another, is either an extension of love or it is not. Perhaps you are thinking that love cannot be that simple. But it is that simple. Every word that we speak, every gesture, every action, and every thought is either an extension of love or it isn't. The impulse to search for love is always present in us, and if we are truly an extension of the Love out of which we were born, then we shall attract that Love back into our lives. Whatever we give out, we receive back. That is the way life works.

If our interior spiritual life has become an exercise in narcissism, in self-satisfaction, then we have veered off the path of love. What is the *intent* of our words and actions? The intention is really the key. If our intention is to extend love to others, then we feel filled with the glory and peacefulness of knowing that we are serving as an example of Infinite Intelligence that brought life here to Earth.

We are Spirit's messengers. We are the voice that speaks, the hand that reaches out, the arms that hug, and the strength that can inspire others. When we feel united with Spirit, we know love, and when we know love, we know that we are one—one heart, one mind, one soul – with ALL that is.

CHAPTER 16

Lighting Your Spiritual Passion

Chapter 16

Lighting Your Spiritual Passion

*Only Spiritual Passion, Great Spiritual Passion,
Can Set a Life on Fire.*

When I strike a match to light our campfire tonight, the magic of fire really makes an impression on me. I believe that natural laws of the cosmic universe operate everything, including fire. But it feels like magic when I strike that match tonight! We had waited a long time to burn this wood that we deemed sacred; we had hauled it 3,000 miles, trusting that it was important.

Seated on a bank of the Colorado River, surrounded by fertile California farmland and enveloped by the sound of the coyotes' nighttime calls across the river valley, I feel like it could be any time in human history. This sense of timelessness fills me with a strong awareness of oneness—that all living things are inexorably connected. I feel like a tiny flea in the universe of life as I view the final deep pink streaks of sunset fading to darkness. The geese are settling into the riverbanks for the night, beavers navigate the islands as they head back toward their dams, and a flycatcher has been plying up and down, up and down, the

LIGHTING YOUR SPIRITUAL PASSION

river, searching for the last morsels of evening insects skimming the mirror-smooth surface of the clear blue Colorado.

We have trucked the small, yellow birch fire logs, cut from a fallen tree at Temple Heights Spiritual Camp, nestled on the shore of Maine's magnificent Penobscot Bay, all the way here to Blythe, California. And tonight, their almost instant combustion warms and lights my soul. From coast to coast, the inspiration of Spirit is always with me. And there is always something about striking a match to light a campfire that settles me into an open invitation for spiritual connections. Being seated outdoors, wrapped in the sounds of nature under the open sky, brings forth a primal connection to everything. Such occasions are wonderful times to honor and receive the blessings of Spirit.

As I stare into the fire, my eyes seem to glaze as my mind tries to expand to encompass the magnificence of creation. Magnetically, I am drawn back, over and over again, to the incomprehensible power of Spirit's love for each of us. Striking that match somehow reminds me of the power of conception, when passion ignites to create each one of us—just as we are now, in this moment. Our opportunity to serve as messengers, to be of spiritual service while bringing warmth and light to others, was struck at the moment of our conception—just like the match.

Fire has warmth and light; so does love. Fire demonstrates passion...so does love. The firelight reflects off the water, warming our hands and faces as we sit in silence. Fueled by wood grown in Maine soil, my bone marrow seems to warm to the invitation of opening the door to Spirit. I close my eyes and, at this moment, *I am peace.*

Lighting Your Spiritual Passion

When I finally return from my sacred space, mentally coming back to the riverbank where I had placed my body earlier, the fire is all I see in the deep darkness. The coyotes have stopped howling, and Nature has settled, in preparation for sleep. Peacefully, I wait for a sign from Spirit...and a light, way up the river, becomes noticeable. It is not moving and it is very dim. I wait for the light to come closer to me. It does not move. Just as Spirit does at times, it sits very still and patiently waits for me to respond. I am the one who needs to move closer. I am the one who needs to mobilize myself into closer alignment so that I can view the space around me (my life) more clearly. Spirit exudes patience; it is up to me to light the spiritual passion to move in closer.

It is a lovely evening of relaxed silence, thinking, and just being. The air is heavy with the presence of Spirit—we are One. In times like this, we are being refueled—we are being readied for action. And action requires amassing of energy until we feel passionate. Passion, like fire, can light our spiritual fuse. How do you create the passion in your life to propel you deeper into spiritual connections? How do you set the stage to meet Spirit face to face? Waiting for random inspiration doesn't always work. If connecting with Spirit is important, then it is important to understand how to do it and to plan for such opportunities.

The next morning we packed up and drove back into Arizona. But I kept thinking about the fire—about the wood that was carried cross-country for a special purpose: to bring Spirit along for the ride. My husband and I first met at the Temple Heights Spiritual Camp; it is a very magical place for us. We knew that wood grown on that Maine land would

LIGHTING YOUR SPIRITUAL PASSION

bring passionate energy forward when it was ignited; we had savored that firewood until the "right" moment. When the fire was lit, we were both transformed and led deeper into Spirit. The next morning we departed feeling spiritually regenerated and inspired.

A few days after we'd driven back to our Arizona home, a card arrived from someone whom I had never met. It was a lovely card, saying thank you for some of my writings. A most appreciated gesture it was! But when I studied the photo on the front of the card—hot, steaming, liquid orange-red lava was flowing off a cliff and into the ocean—I realized that this was an image of passion! This boiling liquid, touching and transforming and rebuilding as it flowed, was truly the visual epitome of passionate energy flowing. Seeing it intensified my passionate desire to write, write, write.

When we need to rebuild or to create new territory in our life, we must amass the energy to light our passion. And then we need to let our passion flow, like the lava, steady and without ceasing, forward into building and creating what we want our lives to be. Islands have been formed from red hot lava flowing into the oceans. I like the thought of being like an island, surrounded by cool, invigorating water while being a resting place for others.

What is your internal fuel? How do you light your creative fire? How do you amass the energy to be a flow of Spirit out into world?

My husband recently built an in-ground fire pit in our backyard, and it has been blessed and consecrated for spiritual work. We invited friends to share in a Native American flute and drum blessing ceremony on a full moon. We can view the

Lighting Your Spiritual Passion

fire pit from our window over the kitchen sink. Every time I look out this window, I am reminded of our intention for building the fire pit: to create a sacred space for healing and inspiration. I like seeing the fire pit there; it feels alive and ready to serve. It is a symbol of how we want to live in the world: we want to serve our spiritual passions.

Only passion, great spiritual passion, can set a life on fire.

CHAPTER 17

Marrying the Personality and the Soul

Chapter 17

Marrying the Personality and the Soul

Today I am seated at 7400' elevation in the Kaibab National Forest in northern Arizona. It is mid-November, and the ponderosa pine trees are majestic sentinels, their tops swaying in the wind as they whisper their own melodious language. Each time the wind speed is about to increase, I am forewarned by the music of the 8–10" pine needles as they rub against each other with familiar dance movements, creating songs that echo across the dry 40-acre lake bed in front of me. What a happy aural agreement Nature displays!

I feel like a creature of Nature today, as I nestle deeper into the dropped pine needles, twigs, and cones here on the skin of Mother Earth. Reclining on my red blanket with pen and paper in hand, I am reminded of the natural cycles of life that involve endings and rebirths. Looking up into Father Sky's brilliant display of limitless clear blue, I am showered with rays of sunlight breaking through the umbrella of huge tree arms hovering above. I feel small here—even smaller than the butterflies, the late fall high-desert daisies, and the varieties of small insects that dot the nearby landscape. All of us are fully engaged in discarding and

LIGHTING YOUR SPIRITUAL PASSION

renewing, discarding and renewing. I am discarding that which no longer serves to invigorate my life with new thoughts, new ideas, and new behaviors, and our spiritual connections are renewed through being immersed in the natural world.

Life feels bountiful in this magnificent forest; no one is in sight except my husband, who is sitting quietly on a large stump in the distance. We came here this weekend seeking both solitude and union—solitude for self-reflection and union with Spirit. We are filling ourselves with the glory of Nature as she progresses through the changing seasons. Nature discards that which no longer serves, and replaces it with new life in the spring. The harmonious glories of Nature, moving in complete tandem, are truly wonders to observe.

Elk abound here in the high country, and, in late fall, they are fully engaged in mating rituals. The males issue high-pitched trumpet calls that resound through the forest to summon the females. These shrill cries echo throughout the mountains and deep canyons of this high country. Squirrels scurry, filling winter hoards with pine cones, nuts, and delicious forest bounty. Small birds are busy hiding seeds for winter feasts. Hawks and crows are riding fall's wind currents through the canyons and mountain gorges. Late-turning yellow leaves cling to the aspen branches, waiting for heavy fall rain to send them tumbling to the ground, where they will form a winter blanket for the earth. Small mammals and rodents are running across fields, hoping to escape the eagle's talons, while drowsy flies seem to barely have enough energy for a liftoff. They are all doing "what comes naturally" during this season of transition.

Are we that smart? Are we living our lives "naturally," allowing our lives to progress smoothly from one stage to

Marrying the Personality and the Soul

another, or are we setting up artificial internal barriers? Are our self-expectations based on our natural talents, or are we creating self-expectancies that are not really aligned with our own personalities and soul paths? When we spend years attempting to achieve professional or personal goals, are we deeply satisfied that we stayed with the programs we chose? If you are experiencing deep-seated, lasting joy, then you probably are achieving goals that truly feed your soul and match your personality. You have truly found your path.

But not everyone feels fulfilled; not everyone has found a personal/professional/spiritual path that feels right. There are many people who still find themselves feeling empty after years of committed effort toward achieving goals. The process often involved long hours and financial stress. The efforts were often grueling, and the resulting achievements did not bring the joy that they had anticipated.

When this pattern begins to repeat in your life, where do you turn? Does your life feel empty at times, no matter how hard you try? Do your own self-expectations seem to be mismatched with your personality? Do you have trouble setting and achieving goals, or if you do achieve the goals, do they seem to be less fulfilling than you had imagined? If so, maybe it is time for some deep soul-searching. Perhaps there are some ways to begin rethinking about how to find your life's purpose.

I believe, deeply in my heart, that the purpose of life for each individual can only be discovered when our soul becomes married to our personality. Each unique personality yearns to be wedded to the soul, and that "union" is realized from our total commitment to following our internal leadings or intuition. The

LIGHTING YOUR SPIRITUAL PASSION

process of joining the soul and personality requires honesty about self-motivations, and it requires humility coupled with patience. It is not about a sudden "aha" experience, but about finely honed personal and spiritual awareness.

As your spiritual connectivity sparks, refilling your life with spiritual Light, this connectivity is reenergized through the God-Force. Ask to be guided, look to the Light, and promise to go where the Light leads you. Then follow the nudging, one step at a time. This gradual process will lead you to your own personal truth, and you will discover your life purpose.

We are spiritual messengers—all of us. In the perfection of Infinite Intelligence's scientific and mathematical designs, we have been given the gift of free will to explore the philosophical depths of our spiritual roots. Do you feel a longing to live a life that has deep meaning? How will you find your path of spiritual fulfillment? What part of the "mystery" of spirituality will you help to illuminate for others? How will you, both for yourself and as a mentor for others, move out of fear and into deeper and deeper levels of trust? What do you have to offer that will make the world a more compassionate and loving place?

The answer to all of these questions comes from offering ourselves up to Spirit's work. If you are feeling misaligned or askew, ask—over and over—to be guided back onto your own path. Keep the Light in front of you and see yourself walking into it—not once, not twice, but again and again. Spiritual depth is not a goal; it is a process that takes a profoundly deep level of internal focus and commitment, finely honing our human comprehension and understanding.

You will know you have truly found the right path because your soul will hum. You will feel like the towering ponderosa

Marrying the Personality and the Soul

pine trees that swayed in the breeze above me. You will vibrate with the energy of knowing about that which brings a sense of totality to you. You will feel tall, empowered. You will hum with internal singing, and you will *know* the glory of being "filled with the Spirit." And others will know that you are experiencing this knowledge because you will radiate the Light of Spirit into the world. You will become happy, and they will respond to that happiness. Joy is contagious—everyone wants it! Share the joy of Spirit with everyone you meet—every day.

When the personality and the soul are wedded in a unified whole, we experience the self as holy because we are filled with the Light that we can reflect out into the world. Do not hide your internal Light, for you are a spiritual messenger.

Ask, "How can I be of service?" Everything else will, in time, fall into place for the union of your personality and your soul, resulting in a wedding of spiritual alignment. This union will become the magnet that will attract more and more abundance to your own "Tree of Life."

As humans, we have an unquenchable thirst for spiritual connections to everything in the physical and spiritual realms. It is no coincidence that many highly respected and very successful spiritual leaders stress setting one's intention, coupled with a deep level of personal commitment, to achieve deeper and higher spiritual connections. They are speaking about the wedding of the personality to the soul; they are speaking about the two working in harmony. When your deeply rooted spiritual beliefs become grounded in trust, your ongoing commitment will unroll the joys of life in front of you, laying the path for you follow. May you walk your path of life in beauty!

CHAPTER 18

Feeding the Soul with Reverence

Chapter 18

Feeding the Soul with Reverence

As we become enveloped by the spirit of the holiday season here in America, Christian and Jewish symbols decorate our landscape. While preparations for Christmas and Hanukkah celebrations accelerate, materialism often seems to be the driving force in our media, urging us to spend more and more money with the promise of increased happiness. But we know that happiness is not achieved through possessing material objects. Happiness comes from feeling a deep connection with God—a personal relationship.

The heart and soul of religion is reverence, and during the holiday season, we have many opportunities to be brought into a sense of "being reverent." Reverence is a feeling or an attitude of deep respect, love, and awe, especially for something sacred. It is the feeling of kneeling in worship or raising our voices in praise as we sing beautiful holiday hymns and songs about love, family, community, and God's magnificence. Who among us can hear "The Hallelujah Chorus" sung by the Mormon Tabernacle Choir without your eyes being stung by tears? How many Christmas Eves have we spent huddled around the television, anticipating feeling close spiritual connections with

LIGHTING YOUR SPIRITUAL PASSION

family while listening to those magnificent choral voices ringing through the Mormon Tabernacle's ceiling rafters in Salt Lake City? That is reverence—feeling like we are in love with the God-connection. We become transformed through grace.

Reverence is a perception of the soul, and reverence happens when we allow ourselves to be completely immersed in spiritual connectivity. We offer ourselves—with no holding back—"up" to the experience. We become the offering, and in turn, we are given the gift of experiencing reverence. Sarah Ban Breathnach wrote a definition of reverence that leaves me speechless:

Reverence is that altered state of consciousness
when you feel awe and wonder
because you know you are in the presence of Spirit.
Reverence enwraps you in perfect peace
because there is no past and no future,
only the present moment,
and you are one with heaven and earth.

There is no distinction between body and soul. Breathnach's definition is about joining—about becoming "One with Spirit" as we come full circle, back to join with that magnificent Force out of which we were created. When we enter into a state of reverence, we are transformed into perfection. We experience ourselves as "perfect." That feeling of being whole—complete in that moment, just as we are—is truly beautiful. It is the sense of coming Home, because it connects us with our own "spiritual birth."

We yearn to feed our souls through reverent experiences. The holidays inspire a desire in us to feel deeply reverent.

Feeding the Soul with Reverence

Music, gifts, giving and receiving, biblical passages, cold nights and warm fires, family dinners, trips to visit friends, holiday lights, movies and theater productions, school plays and concerts combine into a seemingly endless stream, filling our calendars. The reverence that such things can inspire often dissipates in the stress of holiday activities. We want to connect to a deeper level of spirituality, but it often becomes increasingly difficult to do so amidst the holiday hustle and bustle. We are bombarded with distractions, obligations, and expectations of ourselves and others.

Then, after the celebrations have passed and we finally have time to settle down for a deep winter's rest, many people report feeling profound depression. Why do so many people feel so alone and sad in January, and why does that month display the highest levels of abuse, suicide, and divorce? Perhaps it's because, even though the media displayed image after image of unsurpassed laughter and happiness in the previous weeks, the soul has not been fed with reverence.

Spiritual reality is sometimes a hard concept to hang onto in December when we are engulfed with superficial, materialistic promises of how much love we will receive if we give the "perfect" gifts. It is important to make time for reverent experiences.

In our home, my husband and I do not buy Christmas gifts for each other. Instead, we discuss a place that we might like to visit together, and we usually plan an outing that we hope will be spiritually inspirational. We believe that our deepest soul satisfactions are achieved through planned spiritual excursions that immerse us in nature, offer us an experience to work with master teachers, or place us in settings deemed to

LIGHTING YOUR SPIRITUAL PASSION

be sacred by our ancestors. We love to feel the earth under our feet, to sit in shallow rivers flowing through the desert, to stand breathless on high mountains, to walk through melting glaciers, to watch ocean islands shrouded in fog, or to sit in the rear pew of a little community church or in a magnificent cathedral as we listen to the silence. These are our holiday gifts to each other—the opportunity to be together in settings where we can open ourselves to growing deeper spiritual roots, feeding our souls with reverence. Then, when the holidays are over, we have that deeper internal foundation to access when life becomes noisy again—and it always does!

Set aside time for Spirit. Make time for God. Build spiritual communication lines into your day. Ask to be guided, and ask for patience with those relationships you find challenging. We have the ability to reflect, to learn, and to change. If the holidays fill you with a sense of just wanting to hide until they are over, do not be too hard on yourself. But do try something new this year; make time for yourself with Spirit each day, in a very committed way, in a space that you have sanctified or made sacred. Honor your soul's hunger for spiritual connections.

For instance, you might offer ten minutes at 9:00 p.m. as you sit in a chair in a darkened bedroom while holding an object that has sacred significance for you. Would you set aside ten minutes each day if you were promised that your life would unfold more smoothly and efficiently? If you knew that solutions to your problems would appear more readily and that you would feel more certain of which direction to go, would you give up just ten minutes per day to begin to set the energy in motion? I bet you would!

Feeding the Soul with Reverence

As you begin to offer your problems and gratitude back to that which created you, Spirit will step in closer and closer and you will increasingly feel more guidance and inspiration. I know. Be persistent and patient—Spirit rarely moves on our schedule. The ten prayerful minutes each day will not change God, but they *will* change *you*. Like a magnet, you will begin to attract that reverence which you seek. And remember, there is always something that you can express gratitude for each day. You are the one who must accept the responsibility of keeping the lines of spiritual communication open. The phone line is connected, but you have to make the call; you are the one who will issue the summons.

One of the greatest gifts I ever received came from a friend about fifteen years ago when I was going through a transition around the holidays that seemed to be dragging on and on. She simply said, "Would you like me to pray with you?" I had often heard people say that they would pray *for* someone, but the offer to pray *with* me really was a surprise. "Yes," I replied. She took my hands in hers, looked heavenward (where her Baptist God resided), and asked God to guide me into a path of service and giving that would be both useful and gratifying.

I felt like "the heavens parted" when I willingly offered my hands to place in hers. It was the combination of her prayerful desire to be of service and my willingness to allow her to ask "her" God, on my behalf, for guidance for me. My life began to move, to open, and to reveal opportunities that filled me with profound gratitude and joy. Recently, some fifteen years later, I thanked her. She didn't remember the exact event, but I do. She brought an experience of reverence to me as a gift, and I share this story because some of

LIGHTING YOUR SPIRITUAL PASSION

you will probably encounter someone who is feeling blue during the holidays. Even if it feels like taking a risk, ask if that person might be willing to pray with you. It might be the greatest holiday gift you could offer. Sometimes a seemingly simple gesture can be the most intimate and transforming experience. Follow your heart and you will be led into similar opportunities.

Making time for reverence, to be present with and in awe of spiritual mystery, even when our holiday schedules are packed full, is really empowering. Offer your reverence and you will be rewarded with gifts beyond your wildest imaginings. You will flow through life more peacefully when you volunteer to respond to the inner voice that often speaks in mysterious ways. Over time, your persistence and patience will lend strength to your intention to have a closer relationship with God.

As you ask to be led forward, remember that prayer is hope in action with no boundaries. Hope can be static; but when you combine your hope with prayer, you have given it wings, propelling it into action. Setting aside time to be with the Creator is the greatest gift you can give yourself.

CHAPTER 19

The Love We Give Away
Is the Only Love We Keep

Chapter 19

The Love We Give Away Is the Only Love We Keep

The love we give away is the only love we keep. What do others see when they look at you? Do they see a rested, calm, peaceful person who appears to operate from a solid spiritual foundation, or do they see a tired, lonesome person who feels stressed, without much hope for a better future? Do you exhibit an attitude of trust and assurance, or are you concerned about scarcity? Do you feel safe enough inside to give love freely to all?

The love we give away is the only love we keep. If you have love emanating from your soul, then you probably understand that the opposite of scarcity (or lack) is not abundance; it is *enough*. Trusting that there is always enough enables more sharing. If you resonate with this idea, then you probably share love freely. Perhaps you are viewed as an individual who is filled with love and compassion in your community, at work, or in your family. If so, you understand that the only love we keep is the love we give away. You demonstrate spiritual wisdom.

LIGHTING YOUR SPIRITUAL PASSION

The love we give away is the only love we keep. Working to lessen and to eventually eliminate prejudice, anger, mistrust, and hatred is about working to bring ourselves into closer alignment with our Higher Power. It is about working to offer more love out into the world, expressing compassion to those who often seem to deserve it least.

The love we give away is the only love we keep. A beginning step might be to really listen to others as they talk. Did you really listen to each person who spoke to you today? Did you offer feedback? Did they truly feel heard? As each of us is filled with a sense of expanding love, this love filters out into the world. What would happen in each of our homes, our churches, our schools, our governments, and our personal lives if we approached every interaction from a position of love?

The love we give away is the only love we keep. Love allows life to flow more freely. By offering more love, perhaps we might stop trying to control where life is going and allow life to flow. This does not mean that we would stop trying to achieve goals, that we would lie down and wait. It means that we would keep creating, keep moving forward in the directions that we feel drawn, while allowing Spirit to guide and mold the process, bringing increased experiences of synchronicity into our daily life. Days would become more interesting as we allowed life to take its own course. When we can approach life from a position of love, we can be more productive and enjoy the process of being greeted with mysterious events that we never anticipated. Synchronicity would flourish!

The love we give away is the only love we keep. When we respond in ways that are filled with love, we make contributions to the world that meet the world's needs and our own

The Love We Give Away Is the Only Love We Keep

needs at much higher levels. Things flow smoothly and work in better balance. Creativity would function at a higher level to solve the world's problems. Look internally and examine your understanding of love.

The love we give away is the only love we keep. Seek and you will find. Look within your own heart for fulfillment, for it is only when we take care of ourselves that we can nurture others. It is only when we love ourselves that we can infuse others with love. If living one's own life is difficult, then trying to live with another person will be incredibly difficult. Why? Because relationships are the greatest challenges we face. Relationships are also our greatest growth opportunities.

The love we give away is the only love we keep. When we live life expressing love, we live a life that is infused with passion. That passion works like a magnet to create more wonderful experiences. Passion ignites the love we feel and the fire warms others. The energy of love that we emanate changes everything around us for the better.

The love we give away is the only love we keep. Person by person, moment by moment, we can change the world. All of the inner reserves of LOVE are easily accessible and require spending a few moments each day outside of the swirling demands of daily life. Love requires that we understand and appreciate the value of time alone for meditation and prayer, and for expressing gratitude back to the Source. Fill yourself with the joy of giving and receiving love in ways that are passionate, heart-connected, and rewarding. Love grows by giving.

CHAPTER 20

The Mystic Map Within

Chapter 20

The Mystic Map Within

When we are with someone whom we love and trust, our heart is open. This openness brings opportunities for new awareness about old situations and difficult issues, and it surrounds us with hope for the future. We are in love with the gift of life, with the expectation that all is well.

Knowing that we are always safe implies knowing that we are divinely guided and that there is a mystic map within each one of us that is always guiding us, showing us the way. In order for us to read that map, our inner light must be burning with a flame and must be brilliant enough for us to discern the markings on the map. Our hearts must be open so that we can trust this intuitive guidance, our Higher Power.

When we are still and trust, this inner light feels illuminated. We no longer live in dark indecision, but in knowing the bright Light of Spirit. The native peoples say that our feet are on "the red path." How do we find that path? Who will guide us? And how many of us are able to live in ways that bring us closer to the heart of the Great Mystery? How long does it take to develop the integrity, the desire, the yearning, and the trust to live in close relationship with Spirit?

LIGHTING YOUR SPIRITUAL PASSION

When we strive to live each day with an open heart, we discover within ourselves the Mind that governs everything. We are continuously becoming; we are continuously being created. We can choose to drift with the events that are going on around us, or we can choose to interact. We can choose to cling to that which no longer serves our lives, or we can choose to let go, even when it hurts.

When we are open to progress in our lives, when we plan and work toward opening ourselves to our internal guidance, there is a response. Often we can hardly believe the unfolding, yet believe we should, because we participate in the creation of our dreams. When we dare to expect an increasing "unfoldment" of energy, creativity, and love in our lives, it does occur. Listen to the Inner Presence for guidance and inspiration; it will come forward. Then you can decide when to act. Spiritual experience comes in the stillness of the soul, when the outer voice is quiet. It is a quickening of the inner person (Higher Power) to an internal reality.

When was the last time your soul quickened in response to making a connection with Spirit? Think and remember. This is how we grow deeper into spiritual connectivity, becoming more ourselves. We need to choose to live our own destiny. Focusing on our heart's desire to experience our divine essence allows the natural process of divine awakening to unfold. It is not a matter of luck; it is a matter of committed intention. Always remember to "ask and you shall receive." Maybe not at the time you were hoping for, or in the way you wanted, but you shall receive.

It takes great courage and strength to move deeper into self-awareness. It doesn't happen by accident, and it doesn't

The Mystic Map Within

happen overnight. However, when we trust that there is always help available for the asking, the results feel miraculous. And once we experience how much life opens, how opportunities become prolific, we yearn to help others walk their path of exploration. Excitement and joy are contagious, and they attract more excitement and joy.

Each person's mystic map is different. We can support others' spiritual journeys but no one can do the walk for us. Each person travels the spiritual path in a unique way. Just look at how many religions there are in the world; each person must choose a path and travel at his or her own speed.

How do you want to spend the rest of your life? What kind of work do you feel really suited for in today's world? Do you have the courage to keep growing and learning? Examine your personality traits to see if your dreams and goals are a good match for your character. When we can meld our soul's path with our individual personality traits, then we are truly onto something magnificent!

CHAPTER 21

The Fountainhead

Chapter 21

The Fountainhead

Every area of our life experience is open to self-scrutiny. That scrutiny can bring forth positive changes or it can build internal barriers that might seem difficult to overcome. Our internal check-and-balance system comes from a combination of our intellect (mind) and our inner knowing (spirituality). When we have achieved some level of balance regarding mental and spiritual connections (which comes from honest internal evaluation), our bodies' receptors are tuned and prepared to receive powerful spiritual learning experiences.

Neuro-researcher Candace Pert has said that your mind is in every cell in your body. No wonder our intuitive functioning is so accurate! Every cell is involved! By expanding our minds in preparation for deeper spiritual connections, we eliminate a great deal of internal clutter and confusion. We are able to live more within the realm of reality, and can deal with things as they are. When we deal with things as they are, we live within the Truth. We stop self-defeating rationalizations and wishful thinking.

When we know something, we feel a sense of clarity that seems peaceful but can also be frightening. How often we have

LIGHTING YOUR SPIRITUAL PASSION

heard, "It is really better for So-and-So not to know." Is it always better to know than to wonder about something? Can one know too much? The problem comes from the fact that when we know something, we are much less able to hide from the responsibility of responding. There are certainly many times in our lives when it is easier not to know about too many specific details that might bring pain and suffering. However, with spiritual work, exploring the mystery of life often makes us want to keep on going. Many develop a thirst that calls us back to the source of our origin—back to our Creator.

When a spiritual experience (dream, coincidence, sighting) brings forth a connection with a loved one who has gone on, the insight that the personality has survived death often brings feelings of bewilderment and joy, which can include mystery and awe. Science and religion are both talking more and more about the soul and what happens to it when the physical body ceases to live. Physicians are reporting stories by the thousands and science has become increasingly interested. The last time I checked, over 70% of the world's population believes in reincarnation—the repeated return of the soul to earth.

If the visible world is the invisible organization of energy, then perceiving things beyond the normal human ranges of experience is about being connected in deep ways to a living sea of energy. Is Spirit a living sea of energy that possesses intelligence and reasoning powers? And how might this living sea of energy be organized? How does Spirit create order out of chaos?

This brings up a problem in my mind regarding an aspect of formal education. When one spends years within an

The Fountainhead

academic institution, too much of the intuitive can be ignored, stifled, or eliminated from daily life. Of course it is important that we have enough educational background to comprehend the society in which we live and to earn a decent living in a profession of our choice. But most colleges and universities do not stress following one's intuition. Higher education institutions focus on details, on dissecting information, which is about unraveling. Trust, faith, intuition, and integrity seldom enter into classroom discussions.

I believe that *weaving together our spiritual threads of information fashions the garment we wear as our faith*. It seems to me that a freshman in college should be exposed to the possibility that there might be an internal voice guiding him or her toward a career based on his or her personal leading. It is in the development of our inner knowing that we develop wisdom, and that wisdom comes from awareness and understanding. I would ask every college freshman to explore their personal source of inspiration. What is the inspirational fountainhead?

Today I understood exactly what experiencing direct contact with my fountainhead meant as I sat just outside of Acadia National Park (Maine) at Seawall, where thousands of pinpoints of light danced glory hallelujah on the surface of the Atlantic Ocean. The 74-degree temperature was perfect and there was no breeze. The sun glinted off the gentle waves on an incoming tide as silent sailing ships and lumbering lobster boats bobbed on the swells. I could see crew members pulling on sail riggings and lobstermen hauling traps filled with lobsters.

For me, the light on the water today was a quiet miracle. Like so many powerful internal moments, it was bathed in quietude and exuded brilliance. The light had the gift of being

LIGHTING YOUR SPIRITUAL PASSION

both intimately personal and totally universal. The fact that time stands still in these moments of relatedness seemed so simple. "I am that I am," went through my mind. Breathing slowed and I felt enmeshed with the ALL. The next two hours felt long and extended, still and calm, sitting in the warm sun, entranced by the light, on the cool rocks. I was reminded of the delusion of separateness—the idea that one's thoughts and feelings are isolated. Nonsense! We are always a part of the magnificent whole.

This moment of light on the water was a moment of stepping into the exploration of timeless mystery. Humans struggle to embrace the mysterious. Invite the mystery to dinner. Feed it, digest it, talk with it, and leave the door ajar so that it can come and go as a welcome visitor to your table of consciousness. When your knowledge enhances your awe, then you are onto something really BIG. As you enter into direct communication with the mystery, your knowledge will expand and you will grow into new awareness and deeper connection with Spirit. Happy dining!

CHAPTER 22

How Is Your Spiritual Nature Connected to Your "Real" Life?

Chapter 22

How Is Your Spiritual Nature Connected to Your "Real" Life?

Many of us are too busy and too intellectually self-defended to allow small gateways for inspiration to enter.

In order to have our spiritual nature at the forefront in our life, we must be ready to make a shift in consciousness. This is radical work. It is not gentle, it is not passive, and it does not evolve without strenuous effort.

- First we have to commit to becoming that which we yearn to be—a creative aspect of the unfolding of love on planet Earth.
- We must set our intention in a rock-solid foundation by monitoring our thoughts, words, and feelings about every event in our lives.
- Our moral imagination will be strengthened and firmed as we keep reminding ourselves of the spiritual path we have chosen to walk.

There will be times when we try to trick ourselves, when we move out of the reality of the moment and slide back into

LIGHTING YOUR SPIRITUAL PASSION

our previous (and usually ineffective) ways of viewing and responding to the events in our lives. But we always have the opportunity to identify and make adjustments to our thinking and behavior patterns as our spiritual progress evolves.

Yes, we always have a choice in how to think or behave, and it is in these choices that our spirituality is exhibited. We can learn to eliminate knee-jerk reactions to events that bother us. We can choose our responses: thoughtful, spiritually based responses. We can monitor our attention, nurturing and guiding it back to Spirit.

The human mind is designed for limitless liberty. It strives for what is lofty, majestic, beautiful, glorious, exalted. There is nothing too free, too stupendous, too magnificent for the human mind. To search, to explore, to analyze, to imagine, to create—these are the missions of the mind. The mind is where we hear our intuition, our leadings, personal and communal spiritual messages, and, for many, the Voice of God speaking, urging us toward the Light.

George Bernard Shaw, in the play, *Saint Joan*, wrote:

> Joan: "I hear voices telling me what
> to do. They come from God."
> Robert: "They come from your imagination."
> Joan: "Of course. That is how messages
> of God come to us."

Our minds take in information, and the thoughts and behaviors we choose to respond with release a variety of energy patterns. Energy is in constant, vibrating motion. We are constantly sending and receiving it. Energy flows where our attention

How Is Your Spiritual Nature Connected...

goes. As we raise our energetic vibrations, expanding our awareness of the power of positive thoughts and actions, we understand more and more about filling ourselves with the energy of Light. There is a continuous sending and receiving station in Universal Consciousness. Tapping into that station, into that power, is what spiritual work is all about. Every thought moves outward like ripples in a pond, so be careful what you think. As we send out, so we receive. LIKE ATTRACTS LIKE, so it is important to be careful and to monitor our thoughts!

Spiritually speaking, we can change the rate of vibration of our mind and soul to tune into a more refined state of awareness. As we move into deeper levels of connective awareness, consciously working to raise our energies and to open our hearts, we will attract energy that vibrates in sync with our own personal level of awareness. This is why we are often given small glimpses of insight over what might seem like long periods of time. We absorb information that we are ready to comprehend, plus a little more to keep inspiring us to remain on our chosen trail. As we ponder that material, we are growing in awareness, moving gradually into higher and higher realms of enlightenment.

Working with Spirit is a creative process. The subconscious mind registers everything we encounter, so learning to tap into the subconscious is a developmental process. We use many different forms of altered states of consciousness: dreaming, reading, jogging, exercising, listening to music, doing needlework, woodworking, or any other activity that opens us creatively through increased vibration and focus. Through meditation or prayer we can learn to shift our consciousness in a controlled manner.

LIGHTING YOUR SPIRITUAL PASSION

Inside our skulls is a double brain that embraces many different ways of processing, knowing, and experiencing information. There are thousands of exercises to stimulate and develop spiritual connectivity. In my spiritual development classes, we explore some of these; what works for one class member might not work for anyone else in the room. For some, a particular fragrance, such as gardenia, can stimulate communication with the spiritual realm. For others, massaging the energy centers in the base of the skull before inviting an altered state of consciousness is very helpful. *Some people have to see things before they believe in them, and others have to believe in them before they can see them.* Each person is different and will come into deeper levels of spiritual connectivity and communication in their own individual way.

The searching process eventually opens into the developmental process, which then leads forward into daily spiritual practices. The most meaningful practices are those that are self-chosen and self-designed. Again, we are required to choose, to exert our free will. Only you know—in some deep internal place—what your soul desires.

Spiritual development is a pilgrimage about healing. The only two things in life that hold us back from all that we dream of being are fear and guilt. A spiritual path washes away fear and guilt, and we arrive into a cleaner and clearer sense of awareness. We heal guilt and fear as we move into an expanded state of true freedom and evolving magnificence. By choosing a spiritually based road in life, we can clarify our unsettled confusions and unresolved issues, which impede spiritual growth (and often arise during the pilgrimage process). Native Americans call this a vision quest. Celts would

How Is Your Spiritual Nature Connected...

call it a quest about using your own creativity to encounter your creator.

Spiritual work is a radical act because it is about finding wholeness and healthy autonomy. We are meant to feel fulfilled, to experience joy, love, and connection, but spiritual growth is not always easy or comfortable because it involves severing ties with outmoded hierarchies in your life. The journey is about the creation of a very personal process of transformation that works for you.

We each have an individual, indisputable, indestructible connection to the Divine. Energy flows where our attention goes, and I believe that our attention—personal, communal, global and universal—is flowing toward spiritual wholeness. As we heal guilt and fear, we move forward into deeper levels of awareness. We are our souls' keepers, and our real life is our spiritual life.